INVESTING SMART

INVESTING SMART

How to Pick Winning Stocks with *Investor's Business Daily*

DHUN H. SETHNA

McGraw-Hill
New York   San Francisco   Washington, D.C.   Auckland   Bogotá
Caracas   Lisbon   London   Madrid   Mexico City   Milan
Montreal   New Delhi   San Juan   Singapore
Sydney   Tokyo   Toronto

Library of Congress Cataloging-in-Publication Data

Sethna, Dhun H.
   Investing smart : how to pick winning stocks with Investor's
business daily / Dhun H. Sethna.
      p.   cm.
   Includes bibliographical references and index.
   ISBN 0-07-057872-9 (pbk. : alk. paper)
   1. Investments.   2. Stocks.   3. Investment analysis.
4. Investor's business daily.   I. Title.
HG4521.S4557   1997
332.63'22—dc21   96-51816
                                                          CIP

McGraw-Hill

A Division of The McGraw·Hill Companies

   2 3 4 5 6 7 8 9 0   DOC/DOC   9 0 2 1 0 9 8 7

ISBN 0-07-057872-9

*The sponsoring editor for this book was Susan Barry, the editing
supervisor was Patricia V. Amoroso, and the production supervisor was
Claire B. Stanley. It was set in Fairfield by Dina E. John of McGraw-
Hill's Professional Book Group composition unit.*

Printed and bound by R. R. Donnelley & Sons Company.

This publication is designed to provide accurate and authoritative
information in regard to the subject matter covered. It is sold with the
understanding that the publisher is not engaged in rendering legal,
accounting, or other professional service. If legal advice or other expert
assistance is required, the services of a competent professional person
should be sought.
   *—From a declaration of principles jointly adopted by a committee
   of the American Bar Association and a committee of publishers.*

This book is printed on recycled, acid-free paper
containing a minimum of 50% recycled, de-inked fiber.

To my wife, Virginia,
Jonathan and Judith,
and Diana

And to
Jay Benoist,
who introduced me to
Investor's Business Daily

CONTENTS

Part Two. Analysis of the Stock Market

CHAPTER FOUR. ECONOMIC VITAL SIGNS   77

CHAPTER FIVE. THE PSYCHOLOGY OF MARKET BEHAVIOR   113

CHAPTER SIX. THE FUNDAMENTAL VALUES OF CORPORATIONS   129

CHAPTER SEVEN. THE INTERNAL STRUCTURE OF MARKETS

QUICK-SCAN INDEXES

QUICK-SCAN INDEX 1

Indicators reported in *Investor's Business Daily*

QUICK-SCAN INDEX 2

QUICK-SCAN INDEX 3

QUICK-SCAN INDEX 4

HOW TO USE
INVESTOR'S BUSINESS
DAILY **FOR:**

FOREWORD

The story of *Investor's Business Daily* is worth retelling. In the fall of 1982, when one of the greatest bull markets in history was getting under way, Alan MacGregor was poring over the major national financial newspapers on a plane trip home from Chicago to Los Angeles. No matter how he went through them, he could not put his finger precisely on what had happened the day before on Wall Street—which stocks were moving and which were not. Alan was then director of institutional marketing for my securities research firm, William O'Neil & Co., which had been publishing premier research for close to 20 years for institutional clients.

"Bill," he asked me with frustration in our office, "why can't we use our unique computer database on the stock market and the economy, which is the best research tool of its kind, to create something that the other newspapers out there just cannot do, something that would give investors all the data they would need, and then some?" It was an intriguing idea, one that kept turning over in my head. Two weeks later I called Alan into my office and spread out a mock-up of what was to become *Investor's Business Daily*. "Al," I recall saying, "I think we can do it!"

The result has been called a journalistic revolution. And for over a decade, in letters and at my seminars, from youngsters and from market-scarred veterans, from tens of thousands of readers from all walks of life, from busy people who need superior information for business and investment decisions, we keep hearing the same thing: They just don't know how they ever got along without *Investor's Business Daily*. For some, a day cannot begin without it. Others have told us that it has given them a whole new outlook on investing, that they no longer subscribe to the old newspapers that never did them any good, and that for the first time in their lives they are making money—serious money—and keeping it.

I hear the same thing about the book that I wrote in 1988 called *How to Make Money in Stocks—A Winning System in Good Times and Bad*, which has gone into a new edition and has sold over half a million copies. And about the audio and video tapes, and the business library and the wall charts that we have produced to help people gain more understanding about the market and how it works. Over 200,000 people have attended our seminars, and many have come over and over again, to learn how to use our newspaper and its companion chart books, the *Daily Graphs*, to recognize each day's most significant investment message, and then apply it to build and follow a winning portfolio doing their own analysis. This, too, has been gratifying.

Now, to them, we present this guide, *Investing Smart: How to Pick Winning Stocks with Investor's Business Daily*, an additional resource designed to capture the quintessential life of the markets through the charts and tables found only in *Investor's Business Daily*. For novice investors, Part 1 presents an appreciation of the rich heritage and legacy of the investment process, covering the evolution of investment ideas from the turn of the century. There is much to learn from what has happened in the past and why; in the stock market, the same patterns have repeated themselves year in and year out over the decades, and those who fail to recognize the patterns do so at their own peril. Part 2 lays the foundation for sharpening the skills needed to discover the leading industry groups and the winning stocks directly from the signals generated by the variety of monetary, economic, sentimental, fundamental, and technical indicators that are presented every day only in *Investor's Business Daily*.

In simple language, the guidebook shows individual investors how to access the vital information that is critical for their investment decisions, how to monitor the Fed, the business cycle, and the individual stocks, how to understand the signals that identify bullish and bearish market conditions, and how to gain the confidence necessary to buy and sell in the modern markets. The wide range of instruction within its covers becomes apparent by skimming through the Quick-Scan Indexes in the front of the book, the Bibliography at its back, and the references at the end of each chapter.

Like *Investor's Business Daily*, this is a book about doing and discovering, about discovering the thousands of newer companies with revolutionary new ideas and new technologies, and innovative products, that make up what I like to call the New America. Whereas other publications seem to spend more time on running the United States down, *Investor's Business Daily* and this book point out what's put our nation on top, and the companies that have kept it there. Examples of such companies abound in the lists of stocks that make up the unique charts and tables in *Investor's Business Daily*. Unfamiliar as their names may sound to the others, they are well known to our readers. And, after all, it is the discovery of these winning stocks and their trends that smart investing is all about.

William J. O'Neil

ACKNOWLEDGMENTS

The biggest debt of this guidebook is to the people who have made their observations and research available. The manual has been put together from a large number of secondary sources which are abundantly referenced in the text, and to them a debt is acknowledged at the outset.

The primary source, however, has been *Investor's Business Daily* itself. Many of the words and ideas presented in this volume have been derived from those who write each day in *Investor's Business Daily*, and the transcription is too diffuse and too numerous to reference individually in each chapter. This acknowledgment is, therefore, directed to them, especially to Leo Fasciocco, Barbara Benham, Chuck Freadhoff, Lisa Lee Freeman, Sherry Kuczynski, Bernice Napach, James Pethokoukis, and Peter Pfabe, whose writings have been transcribed in these pages. In addition, the following are acknowledged here: Ted Bunker, Brian Deagon, Paul Eisenstein, Janice Fioravante, Cathleen Hays, Carl Horowitz, Jesse Malkine, Claude Marx, Thomas McArdle, Jo Beth McDaniel, Mark Mehler, John Merline, Marilyn Much, Charles Oliver, Paul Sperry, Doug Rogers, Anne Scheck, and Rober Stein.

Sincere gratitude is expressed to Heather Davis and Bill Sileo of *Investor's Business Daily* for giving abundantly of their time, and to Philip Ruppel and Susan Barry of McGraw-Hill for their encouragement and patience. Finally, this book could not have been conceived without the vision and support of William J. O'Neil.

The charts, graphs, and tables in this book are reproduced, with permission, from *Investor's Business Daily*. Exhibit 7.4 is reproduced, with permission, from William J. O'Neil, *How to Make Money in Stocks—A Winning System in Good Times and Bad* (McGraw-Hill, 1988).

INTRODUCTION: THE GREAT CONVERSATION

The first issue of *Investor's Daily*, as it was baptized, rolled off the presses in Los Angeles, Calif., and Somerset, N.J., on April 9, 1984. It was born out of a need to meet the individual "Investor's" demand for a new and different "Business Daily" that would give superior financial information and ideas to enable the modern individual investor to trade successfully in the modern financial markets.

The individual investor lives today in a world that is praised for its superabundant data explosion, making this a unique time in history. Few have dared to say that it is a world in which understanding has been enlarged or enhanced, or that wisdom has at last come into its own! The founder of *Investor's Business Daily* took it upon himself to run against the grain in this information age, and to distinguish all that there *is* to know from what an individual investor *needs* to know. In its creation, he used his knowledge and his intuitions, not so much to encompass the whole financial world, but to distill from that world only those particular essences that would enhance success in investment. New information and ideas that are not found in any other daily newspaper are presented here to help make sense of the markets and to determine what is really happening.

The mind thinks with ideas, not with facts. An idea alters and grows, and often takes a lifetime of experience to comprehend fully. And having a life, an idea can have a history—a past, present, and future. It has been said that there is only one method of transmitting thought, of communicating ideas in a manner that somewhat captures the spirit of the mind, and that that medium is conversation. The implicit and explicit goal of conversation is understanding. Conversations are a forum for the exchange of ideas and have as their express goal to get one's point across, to make a connection between one's thoughts and another person. And it is this very spirit that *Investor's Business Daily* captures as it carries on, every business day, a great conversation with the individual investor.

There seems to be an unfounded assumption that, whereas anybody can read the news, very few can read the financial news. The universal use of information systems and machines, the mystery that modern people have made of numbers and formulas in the financial world, and the magical sense of immense wealth that awaits in the markets has filled the minds of potential investors with reflections of things that they believe cannot be grasped. *Investor's Business Daily* dispels the magic and mysteries of making money, and provides the individual investor with all the economic and financial *information* and *ideas* needed on which to base a judgment.

In its pages are presented the great errors and the great truths of the investment world. But the mission of *Investor's Business Daily* goes much further—it is to assist the investor in grasping the history, politics, psychology, and economics of the financial markets, and to develop that intense unity of mood, and habit of mind, which is needed to form a valid judgment. The stock market has many faces. Much has been learned by observing how the economy and the markets have behaved over certain periods in the past, and it is through these remembrances of markets past that a beginning investor may gain more insight into the market of today.

All the theories in the world come to naught unless they work, and investment theory serves no purpose unless it can help investors make money, and keep what they make. *Investor's Business Daily* guides the investor not only how to predict in which direction the financial markets are going, but also how to acquire and retain profits. The great conversation teaches an investor to evaluate objectively the trends of what is going on in the markets, and yet remain detached from the mainstream to watch the level of expectations, the level of speculation, and the level of confidence that form the heartbeats of market dynamics. The market offers advice to whomever is willing to listen and interpret correctly, and is rewarding to those who are able to discover its perplexing ways. The great conversation also teaches that nothing succeeds worse than success in the stock market. It has been said that prosperity in the market seems to encourage optimism and impatience in about the same degree that adversity discourages enterprise and aspiration!

To the making of books on investment there is no end; a new one calls for justification. This work began as a guide and as a means of helping the fledgling investor find his or her way through some of the pages of *Investor's Business Daily*. It has ended as being a preliminary summation of the issues around which the great conversation has revolved. It stands in relation to *Investor's Business Daily* as a window to a house, tendering a first glimpse into the ideas and understanding organized by that structure.

This manual has little to offer that is not already known to the experienced investor or to the market professional. There is no new ground broken in its pages. It is directed primarily to those who have, from time to time, nurtured a desire to understand the financial markets and trade in them doing their own analyses, but have not found the best resources to instruct them. To them, *Investor's Business Daily* brings an easy-to-understand, reliable, comprehensive source of business, economic, and investment ideas that will begin, and deepen, their perspective of the investment process. For them, this book provides a method, an apparatus of the mind, a technique of thinking to use *Investor's Business Daily* to draw independent conclusions.

This book is the outcome of syntopical reading wherein many sources have been read in relation to one another and to a subject about which they all revolve, and from which a syn-

opsis of the subject has been constructed. It is therefore a dis-
tillation of that which has already been written in different
places over a vast expanse of time. In a sense, then, the references here assembled, and quoted from, are the very heart of
the investment tradition, and in these pages the best minds
tell their stories, often in their own words.

Throughout the history of this nation, investments have
been seen as playing a vital role in its development. The
investment future in the United States remains unlimited,
both for the aggressive individual investor and for his conservative counterpart. The market will always make new highs
because it always has! The founder of *Investor's Business Daily*
designed and created its basic format with a goal, that the
ordinary person who chooses to succeed in this free country
should have the machinery and form of the American investment tradition made available to him or her. It was his intent
that every potential investor have the opportunities of the
markets opened and explained, in simple terms, and that
everyone gain the best information needed, day after day. And
this book is dedicated to his vision.

Dhun H. Sethna

PART
ONE

MASTERING THE
LANGUAGE

Investor's Business Daily is continuously making improvements to bring more value to its investors. Some of these changes have occurred during the publication of this book. Most noticeable are those on the first two pages of the *Daily* where a new three-column format called *To Make a Long Story Short* replaces the *Executive News Summary*. It is a quick and easy-to-read format that makes room for four times the news than before. The column *In Brief* is now called *To The Point* and is significantly enlarged. A new feature called *Computers Made Plain* takes the spot of the popular *Investor's Corner* at the bottom of the first page; the latter is now an expanded section contained within the newspaper and can be located from the Contents box on the first page. The many features of the Nasdaq *Intelligent Tables* discussed in this book will soon be extended to the NYSE *Intelligent Tables*. And exciting improvements are planned for the Mutual Funds section!

HOW TO READ
INVESTOR'S
BUSINESS DAILY

Investor's Business Daily is designed and structured to be an expository financial newspaper whose primary purpose is to convey understanding. Such an approach serves to protect the reader from the common folly of reading too widely but not too well. To begin a guided tour, get a Friday edition from a newsstand. The Contents of each issue are shown in a box at the bottom right corner of the first page, and they list the regular topics that are covered in its pages every business day.

HOW TO READ THE FIRST PAGE:
A NEWS DIGEST

The first page demonstrates very clearly the system of instruction adopted by *Investor's Business Daily,* which is to think in terms of essentials. It abstracts ideas that are selected from the universe of financial data available each day. These ideas provide a sense of the world to come, but they have also deeply influenced the world that has always been. They allow a prediction of the long term from an analysis of the present, and permit an appreciation of the present in the context of the historical past. Here is current information, perhaps a number or an outcome, designed to stimulate a chain of reasoning and debate that has invariably formed the substrate for profitable actions in the markets. Benefits are most commonly realized when current happenings are understood simply, within the framework of the basic nature of financial markets and human psychology, or in the distinguishing characteristics that separate one market from the next, or in the cause-and-effect associations that establish valuation and risk and determine market trends.[1] Often, common sense has proved more useful in the financial world than a plethora of figures. This has meant reading between the lines, asking about the significance of the information presented, and asking what else follows, and what is further implied or suggested.

The first page begins, on the left-hand side, with an *Executive News Summary* which condenses, in fewer than five sentences, the backdrop of the social, political, economic, and business influences that make up the current investing environment. Most of the summaries are expanded into brief discussions on other pages as indicated. The general level of stock prices today is influenced by several complex, diverse, and powerful forces that work either by affecting mass psychology or through direct economic operation. These influences include the swings of the business cycle, the trend of interest rates, the effects of rising inflation, the overall government attitudes toward investment and private enterprise, and the birth and development of new inventions and technologies as they affect old industries.[2] All these forces are seldom pulling stock prices in the same direction at the same time. Nor is any one of them necessarily of vastly greater importance than any other over long periods of time. *The Executive News Summary* presents a daily evaluation of the expressions and interactions of these forces, which have become so necessary in determining the safest course to be followed in the financial markets today.

The column *In Brief* provides one-sentence synopses of new happenings in business such as earnings changes, stock splits, mergers and acquisitions, dividend news, changes in company management, changes in interest rates and tax laws, the appearance of a new product or process, and proposed corporate plans. These items have one thing in common. They are real occurrences and activities that have happened, or are about to happen, in the real world. Here one can begin with a single idea, follow it in the marketplace, and come to a decision that is both logical and accurate. This column ends with *The Markets*, which sums up the closing prices and percentage changes from the previous day's trading on the stock exchanges, and in the currency and credit markets. General news that could potentially affect the economy or the political and business world is condensed under *Washington and World*.

The entire right side of the first page is committed to three comprehensive reports on national, business, or financial issues. Typically, the real news is not in the headlines but behind them. In financial markets, as in human affairs, intentions and results are often separate and distinct. *Investor's Business Daily* seeks to understand and unravel the special circumstances that underlie the news to expose the true economic condition, or fundamental situation, of the financial markets and of specific companies. Along with the abundance of material gratification that is characteristic of our affluent society lies a hidden vulnerability: a pervasive reliance on organized cooperation and interdependence.[3] The modern citizen is rich, not as an individual, but as a member of a rich society.[4] The *National Issues* section is often the forum for discussions of interdependencies in the economic sphere proper, or in the organization of the broader society. *Leaders and Success* looks behind the façade of the world's most dynamic leaders, past and present, to understand the philosophy that drives them, how they organize their time, the lessons they have learned from their own mistakes, and how they get it all done. An *Investor's Corner*, at the bottom of this page, is committed to education and instruction on a broad spectrum of investment subjects ranging from a review of current market conditions, or a discussion on the best current investment strategy, to an analysis of a single important stock that has been presented at the meetings of the New York Analysts.

HOW TO USE *INVESTOR'S BUSINESS DAILY* TO MONITOR MARKET SECTORS

Using the Contents, turn to the page on *Market Charts*. A study of the markets as a whole should be preceded by an assessment of the important *market sectors* which represent the broad areas into which an economy has been conventionally divided. The market sectors reflect the first layer of interaction between the overall economy (i.e., the business cycle) and the markets. They offer a broad look, an overview, of the economy as it stands today, and they reflect the current sentiments and actions of consumers and businesses about the economy and the business markets.

The bottom of the charts page has a table entitled *Market Sector Indexes* that summarizes the performances of the broad areas into which an economy has been conventionally divided (Exhibit 1-1). It is designed to permit swift scanning, and to identify precisely the market sectors that are showing the strongest performance. On certain days of the week, the sectors are ranked by their overall performance in the most recent quarter, and on other days they are listed according to their year-to-date best percentage gain. Hence, looking at the

MARKET SECTOR INDEXES FOR 11/4/96

Sorted Monday, Wednesday & Friday by best % performance in last 3 months. List is sorted Tuesday & Thursday by best % gain year to date. Boldface sectors performed better than NYSE composite yesterday.

SINCE JAN 1	3 MONTH %CHANGE	(★ On Left, Top 4 Indexes Since Jan. 1) (★ On Right, Top 4 Indexes Yesterday)	INDEX	YESTERDAY'S CHANGE	%CHANGE
+23.08%★	+12.53%	JUNIOR GROWTH INDEX	324.23	+ 2.78	+0.86%★
+22.24%★	+ 9.80%	SENIOR GROWTH INDEX	471.00	+ 2.77	+0.59%
+21.23%★	+11.04%	N.Y.S.E FINANCE	332.48	+ 1.78	+0.54%
+21.08%★	+12.41%	BANK INDEX	462.55	+ 2.43	+0.53%
+19.11%	+10.83%	HIGH−TECH INDEX	257.49	− 0.07	−0.03%
+16.00%	+ 8.92%	NASDAQ OTC COMPOSITE	1220.48	− 1.30	−0.11%
+15.68%	+ 6.43%	IBD 6000 INDEX	462.40	+ 0.94	+0.20%
+13.83%	+ 6.31%	N.Y.S.E COMPOSITE INDEX	375.07	+ 1.39	+0.37%
+13.33%	+ 8.23%	U.S. DEFENSE INDEX	238.05	+ 0.41	+0.17%
+13.20%	+ 6.32%	VALUE LINE INDEX	645.13	+ 1.51	+0.23%
+11.95%	+ 3.78%	MEDICAL/HEALTHCARE	1376.86	− 7.75	−0.56%
+11.35%	+ 7.39%	S&P MIDCAP 400 INDEX	242.56	+ 0.13	+0.05%
+ 8.74%	+ 4.15%	DOW JONES TRANSPORTATION	2154.23	+16.71	+0.78%★
+ 7.92%	+ 4.84%	NEW ISSUES INDEX	332.11	− 2.16	−0.65%
+ 7.85%	+ 3.63%	CONSUMER INDEX	324.67	+ 0.52	+0.16%
+ 7.66%	+ 2.11%	DEFENSIVE INDEX	750.31	+ 4.44	+0.60%
+ 6.53%	+ 7.71%	INSURANCE INDEX	324.32	+ 1.64	+0.51%
+ 4.29%	+ 4.22%	AMEX MKT. VALUE INDEX	571.76	− 0.82	−0.14%
+ 1.37%	+ 7.46%	DOW JONES UTILITY	228.48	+ 2.03	+0.90%★
− 0.00%	−10.25%	GOLD INDEX	71.88	+ 0.52	+0.73%★

EXHIBIT 1-1.   The Market Sector Indexes.

order of ranking in this list can indicate the strengths and weaknesses of the current economy.

Each market sector is represented by its index number. The *current* value and the percentage change in value of each index from the previous trading day are shown on the right side of the table. The overall *past* performance (gain or loss) of each sector during the most recent quarter (3 *month % change*) and for the year (*since Jan 1*) are shown on the left of the table. Sectors that have performed better than the S&P 500 during the previous trading day are **boldfaced.** Sectors that are consistently boldfaced over a 2- or 3-week period are the emerging leaders whose stocks are worthy of investment potential. The four top-performing market sectors, year to date, are highlighted by an asterisk (*) in the first column of the table; a similar asterisk in the last column identifies the four top performers of the previous trading day.

It has been known for some time that strength in certain market sectors is associated with certain phases of a business cycle, so that leadership in specific sectors indicates that the financial markets are diagnosing a particular phase of a business cycle. For example, when the economy is expanding and inflation is low, consumer and business confidence rises; consumers spend more, resulting in a rise in the *Consumer Index*. Growth stocks (*Junior Growth Index* and *Senior Growth Index*) and high-tech stocks (*High-Technology Index*) begin to step up. Banks, too, do well (*Bank Index*) when consumers and businesses borrow more to participate in the rising economy. As the market accelerates, companies start to raise capital by issuing a wave of new stock that is absorbed by a willing public. The result is a rise in the *New Issues Index*, which tracks initial public offerings of stock for price performance over the previous 12 months.

Changing leadership in market sectors heralds a change in the business cycle from the current phase into the next. Rising leadership in the defensive sector, for example, with a weakening in the manufacturing and interest-rate-sensitive industries, confirms that the financial markets are recognizing a recessionary environment. On the other hand, the early recovery phase of the economy is characterized by strong activity in the familiar blue chips, the cyclicals, the utilities, and the financial issues, all of which are apt to profit most from the low and declining interest rates that prevail during this phase. Rising consumer spending benefits companies in the housing, retail, leisure, food, and auto industries, which draw their income from expenditures of the household sector. Interest-rate-sensitive market sectors include the *Dow Jones Utility Average*, the *Bank Index*, the *NYSE Finance Index*, and the *Consumer Index*. The housing market, along with autos, is also an interest-rate-sensitive sector of the economy.

Rising leadership in the manufacturing and technology sectors indicates that the financial markets are participating in an expansion boom. Strength in the *High-Technology Index*, *Medical/Health Care Index*, *Junior Growth Index*, and *Senior Growth Index* confirms the expansionary phase. Iron, wood, steel, zinc, and other basics that are the raw materials for car makers, home builders, and manufacturers take off late in an economic recovery when the supply of raw materials fails to keep pace with a real or perceived accelerating demand for them. As manufacturers reach full output in their factories, the demand for raw materials often far outstrips supply so that prices of raw materials can rise substantially. Railroad equipment, machinery, machine tools, and other such capital-goods industries are also late movers in a market cycle; when these groups start rising, the end of a market uptrend is near.

Certain market sectors are so dependent on interest rates that their price movements have been used as an indicator of future movements in interest rates. These sectors are the utilities (*Dow Jones Utility Average*) and the financial groups (*NYSE Finance Index*) such as banks (*Bank Index*), brokerages, insurance groups (*Insurance Index*), and savings and loans. The relationship between utility stocks, especially the electric utilities, and interest rates stems from the heavy borrowing incurred by utilities without the ability to pass on these higher costs to consumers because of the regulation of customer rates. This relationship has weakened recently with deregulations in the utilities industry and lighter borrowing by the utilities. Nonetheless, the relationship still holds, because long-standing and deeply rooted market beliefs have not caught up with changing realities.

The association between utilities and interest rates has resulted in a close relationship between the electric utilities and bond prices. A rising utility index indicates that bond yields are falling. Conversely, a declining index points to rising bond yields. The Dow Jones Utility Average has been both a leading and a coincident indicator of the direction of interest rates. In September 1993, for example, the utility index topped out a month before the bond market peaked and then bottomed out into the most bearish bond market in 50 years. On the other hand, in September 1981, the utility index bottomed at the same time as did bonds. Failure of the Dow Jones Utility Average to move in unison with the rest of the stock market has usually been a clue that a change in the direction of interest rates is imminent, with powerful impacts on the stock market.

Market-sector analysis can be continued on the left side of the *Market Charts* page. Here, next to the three big charts of the general market averages, are seven smaller charts of subindexes that allow key market and economic sectors to be monitored together with the general markets. Some market-sector charts are shown only on certain days of the week. The charts cover consumer demand and spending (*Consumer Index*), inflation (*Gold Index*), the interest-rate-sensitive financial group (*Bank Index*), the defensive securities (*Defensive Index*), the medical (*Medical/Health Care Index*) and technology (*High-Technology Index*) groups, the younger growth stocks (*Junior Growth Index*), and the mature, large-capitalization growth companies (*Senior Growth Index*).

These proprietary charts cannot be found in any other financial newspaper. Together, they paint a comprehensive landscape that allows a comparative valuation of those sectors in the economy that are really leading and those that are the true laggards. The charts facilitate an assessment of the current phase of the business cycle.

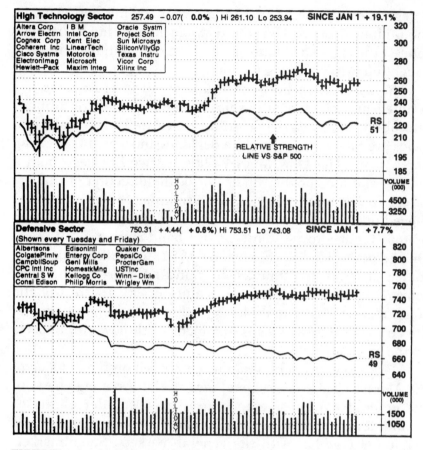

EXHIBIT 1-2.   An Example of a Chart on Market Sectors.

Look at each small chart individually (Exhibit 1-2). The stocks that make up each index are listed separately in a box. This allows one to emulate the performance of a sector. Moreover, each market-sector index is a composite of the many individual stocks that make up the group, and thus acts like a separate, miniature stock market. Since the stocks that make up each sector are known, the value of each market-sector index opens each group to an almost unlimited analysis and scrutiny using the variety of known technical and fundamental indicators that have been tested over decades on the stock market averages and indexes. This is an important point to understand. The market-sector index value is no different conceptually from the value of the closing price of the Dow or the S&P 500, so that it can be analyzed together with its component stocks using the same techniques that have been applied to the market indexes.

The high, low, and close values of each index, the percentage change from the previous trading day, and its overall performance (gain or loss) since the beginning of the year are noted at the top of each chart. All charts have relative strength lines and a current relative strength value to show how each sector is faring relative to the overall market (S&P 500). Volume bars at the bottom of each chart measure the daily supply and demand for the companies that make up each market sector.

HOW TO USE *INVESTOR'S BUSINESS DAILY* TO MONITOR INDUSTRY GROUPS

From market-sector analysis, one can proceed to an interrogation of industry groups. Companies that engage in similar types of businesses, and which therefore have common factors influencing their sales and earnings, are classified into industry groups. Common stocks tend to move in groups, and it has been shown that 49 percent of a stock's price movement is due to major group or subgroup influence.[5] Hence, displaying and monitoring stocks by industry groups can help identify weakening investments faster, and recognize emerging leaders earlier. It has been pointed out that if the right industries could be selected, it would be possible to always be invested in common stocks which were in a rising price trend. New segments in conventional industries have necessitated the evolution of additional groups (subgroups) requiring independent monitoring, since one segment of an industry has been known to rise in price as others in the same industry are simultaneously declining.[6]

Investor's Business Daily has classified stocks into 197 proprietary industry groups. The centerpiece for industry group analysis is the large table on *Investor's Business Daily Industry Prices* (Exhibit 1-3a). These pioneering tables have been specially designed to provide the most comprehensive industry group statistics in the nation. Every day, the groups are ranked from 1 to 197 on the basis of the price performance of all

Investor's Business Daily Industry Prices

197 Industry Groups are ranked 1 through 197 on price performance of all stocks in the industry in the latest 6 months (1 = best performance). Top ten industries in performance yesterday are boldface. Worst 10 are underlined.

Rank This Wk	6 Wk Ago	Last Mo	Industry Name	No. of Stocks In Grp	% Chg Since Jan.1	Daily Chg.
1	1	50	Oil&Gas-Cdn Expl&Prod	119	+38.7	0.0
2	2	2	Oil & Gas-Drilling	18	+83.7	-2.3
3	3	124	**Food-Sugar & Refining**	3	+80.1	+1.1
4	9	148	**Machinery-Thermal Proc**	2	+42.6	+2.2
5	5	133	Food-Flour & Grain	8	+39.0	+1.0
6	11	195	**Retail-Drug Stores**	10	+23.4	+4.6
7	8	13	Oil&Gas-U S Expl&Prod	136	+43.4	+0.3
8	4	132	Insurance-Acc & Health	19	+30.1	+0.3
9	7	103	Real Estate Operations	39	+24.9	-0.7
10	6	93	Finance-Mrtg&Rel Svc	35	+41.6	-0.8
11	15	109	**Finance-Investment Mgmt**	24	+23.3	+1.1
12	14	97	Transportation-Svcs	15	+19.3	-0.3
13	12	138	Hsehold/Office Furniture	26	+23.6	+0.3
14	16	47	Bldg-Mobile/Mfg & Rv	33	+29.8	-0.6
15	13	20	Retail/Whlsle Computers	36	+60.1	-0.1
16	17	118	Banks-Foreign	41	+19.8	+0.3
17	10	6	Oil&Gas-Field Services	39	+41.6	0.0
18	31	155	Banks-Northeast	169	+18.1	+0.7
19	18	83	Computer-Mini/Micro	25	+26.3	-1.1
20	24	8	Oil&Gas-Machinery/Equip	18	+39.9	-0.5

Rank This Wk	6 Wk Ago	Last Mo	Industry Name	No. of Stocks In Grp	% Chg Since Jan.1	Daily Chg.
50	63	139	Banks-Southeast	126	+15.7	+0.1
51	57	63	Finance-Stk&Commrcl	12	+25.5	+0.2
52	55	99	Oil&Gas-Prod/Pipeline	30	+22.3	-0.5
53	34	11	Computer-Memory Devices	45	+20.0	+0.1
54	64	151	Banks-Midwest	113	+14.6	+0.2
55	68	40	Metal-Steel Pipe & Tube	14	+26.3	+0.4
56	56	17	Telecommunications-Svcs	90	+9.8	-1.4
57	58	117	Banks-Southwest	16	+24.1	+0.7
58	49	18	Computer-Software	314	+1.0	-1.0
59	59	169	Finance-Mortgage Reit	43	+16.8	-0.1
60	76	55	Media-Radio/Tv	53	+17.6	-0.6
61	67	194	Food-Misc Preparation	50	+1.9	+0.7
62	36	1	Retail-Apparel/Shoe	62	+45.4	-0.3
63	66	171	Food-Confectionery	7	+17.7	-0.1
64	72	168	Finance-Equity Reit	170	+14.2	+0.2
65	86	162	Oil&Gas-Cdn Integrated	6	+20.4	+0.4
66	51	91	Finance-Investment Bkrs	42	+26.8	+0.8
67	93	185	**Computer-Mainframes**	7	+28.0	+1.3
68	42	24	Elec-Misc Components	60	+11.2	-0.5
69	73	61	Leisure-Hotels & Motels	33	+21.2	-0.4
70	61	3	Comml Services-Misc	175	+22.4	-1.8

Rank This Wk	6 Wk Ago	Last Mo	Industry Name	No. of Stocks In Grp	% Chg Since Jan.1	Daily Chg.
100	100	159	Bldg-Paint & Allied Prds	12	+20.4	+0.2
101	106	98	Chemicals-Basic	15	+19.4	-0.1
102	101	52	Metal Proc & Fabrication	41	+20.5	-0.3
103	124	172	Electrical-Equipment	20	+16.5	+0.5
104	108	140	Office Supplies Mfg	27	+6.6	+0.6
105	107	131	Electrical-Connectors	16	+12.2	0.0
106	117	90	Bldg-Cement/Concrt/Ag	17	+12.5	-0.5
107	70	27	Computer-Local Networks	66	-5.0	-0.6
108	82	10	Telecommunications-Equip	154	+14.3	-0.6
109	122	197	Food-Meat Products	18	-11.7	+0.3
110	126	182	Retail/Wholesale-Food	19	+5.3	-0.1
111	97	135	Media-Newspapers	17	+17.1	+0.1
112	99	130	Energy-Coal	12	+13.1	-0.9
113	105	170	Aerospace/Defense	9	+13.5	+0.5
114	112	16	Computer-Integrated Syst	56	+5.9	-1.0
115	120	19	Comml Svc-Engineering/Rd	21	+3.9	-0.8
116	91	21	Leisure-Gaming	86	+13.1	-1.0
117	121	144	Finance-Publ Inv Fd-Frm	148	+6.7	0.0
118	119	173	Bldg Prod-Wood	17	+7.3	-0.7
119	114	188	Comml Svcs-Printing	20	-7.7	-0.9
120	130	45	Machinery-Const/Mining	11	+41.5	0.0

Rank This Wk	6 Wk Ago	Last Mo	Industry Name	No. of Stocks In Grp	% Chg Since Jan.1	Daily Chg.
150	146	29	Leisure-Products	68	+4.4	-0.4
151	158	80	Office-Equip & Automatn	15	+4.6	+0.3
152	159	58	Elec-Scientific Instrum	42	+0.8	+0.3
153	141	192	Tobacco	11	+0.5	-0.6
154	153	122	Machinery-Farm	10	+4.5	-0.3
155	151	113	Household-Appliances	14	+3.1	-0.2
156	138	57	Retail-Restaurants	138	+1.4	-0.2
157	162	114	Utility-Telephone	22	-7.2	+0.8
158	166	184	Insurance-Brokers	9	+1.9	+0.7
159	142	147	Leisure-Photo Equip/Rel	18	+8.2	-1.8
160	167	107	**Telecommunctns-Cellulr**	35	-3.7	+1.4
161	168	149	**Media-Cable Tv**	32	-16.1	+1.2
162	163	94	**Leisure-Services**	44	+6.7	+1.6
163	154	23	Medical-Biomed/Genetics	159	-3.7	-1.2
164	170	30	Transport-Air Freight	14	+20.5	+0.8
165	127	180	Media-Periodicals	17	-14.7	-0.6
166	169	28	Steel-Specialty Alloys	16	+9.8	-0.2
167	145	34	Medical-Products	161	-4.8	-0.8
168	184	85	**Auto Mfr-Domestic**	4	+9.9	+2.1
169	177	167	Computer-Optical Recogtn	22	-13.5	+0.5
170	173	145	Steel-Producers	23	-12.7	+0.4

EXHIBIT 1-3a. Industry Groups.

**Groups With The Greatest %
Of Stocks Making New Highs**

Retail-Drug Stores	30%
Oil&Gas-Intl Integrated	20%
Soap & Clng Preparatns	18%
Oil&Gas-Cdn Integrated	17%
Finance-Investment Mgmt.............	17%
Insurance-Diversified	14%
Food-Flour & Grain	13%
Medical-Drug/Diversified	13%
Household-Textiles Furns	13%
Transportation-Ship......................	13%
Auto Mfrs-Foreign..........................	13%
Banks-Foreign	12%

EXHIBIT 1-3*b*.   Industry Groups.

stocks in an industry over the latest 6 months. The rank position of each group this week, the previous week (*last week*), and 3 months ago are shown in the first three columns of the table. The top 10 industries with the best performance during the previous day's trading are highlighted in the table by **boldfacing** to identify where the current strength of the market lies, and the worst 10 current industry performers are underlined. The boldfacing shows very clearly the emergence of a new leading group or continued strength in the existing leadership. A group that is persistently underlined is probably under strong selling pressure.

The 197 industry groups are valued by a proprietary price-based Group Index using 1984 as the base year (January 1, 1984 = 100). Each industry Group Index is a composite of the many individual stocks that make up the industry group. Every day, the closing price for each Group Index during the previous day's trading is computed in percentage terms to allow precise comparison of one group's performance with another's. The percentage changes in performance over the previous day (*Daily % Chg*) and from year to date (*% Chg since Jan 1*) allow identification of those groups ranking in the top quartile in performance. The strongest stocks in these strongest groups may then be investigated for potential investment. The table also records the number of companies in each group to show the breadth and the extent of competition within an industry.

The top industry *Groups with the Greatest % of Stocks Making New Highs* during the previous day's trading are separately identified in a box (Exhibit 1-3b) adjacent to the Industry Price table. Both the table and the box can be scanned very quickly each day to identify the strongest current industry groups. The individual stocks that have made the new highs in a leading industry group are listed on a separate page in a table entitled *New Price Highs*, which can be located under *New Highs and Lows* from the Contents.

Every day, a tabular profile of the leading companies in an industry group is displayed in a chart called *Industry Group Focus* at the bottom of the page of *Companies in the News* (Exhibit 1-4). In addition to the proprietary earnings per share, accumulation/distribution, and relative strength rankings, the profile includes important fundamental information on each company: P/E ratios, including high and low values over the past 5 years; the supply of shares (float); the risk (beta) value; the percentage changes in the last quarter's earnings and sales compared with the same quarter a year earlier; and the net percent profit margin, return on equity (ROE), and long-term percentage debt, each calculated annually. This

INDUSTRY GROUP FOCUS

Lilly Industries is a leading member of the Chemicals – Specialty group
14 stocks are shown by total of EPS Rank and Relative Price Strength
o after symbol means OTC; a means Amex; * Calculated annually

Rank	Stock	Trade Symbol	EPS Rnk	REL STR	Acc Dis	Recnt Price	% off High Price	PE Ratio	5yr PE HI-lo		Shrs Outstd (mil)	Avg. DlyVol (100s)	Last Qtr EPS	Last Qtr. Sales	Net % Profit Margin*	Return on Equity*	% Debt*	Bet
1	Zoltek Cos Inc	ZOLT o	99	96	B	27.88	41	77	131	16	15.9	2535	+200	+540	19.2	19.0	65	+1.69
2	Mining Svcs Intl Corp	MSIX o	97	92	B	10.75	38	17	225	6	6.2	43	+ 40	+ 51	17.3	28.1	3	+1.93
3	Macdermid Inc	MACD o	95	89	B	104.00	..	18	18	10	2.8	19	+ 64	+ 39	10.0	18.4	109	+0.03
4	Airgas Inc	ARG	91	84	B	22.63	11	34	43	20	64.5	1137	+ 21	+ 40	8.2	18.7	163	+0.61
5	McWhorter Technologies	MWT	93	76	C	19.13	5	16	23	12	10.6	113	+ 40	+ 5	6.0	16.6	27	+0.80
6	Sybron Chemicals Inc	SYC a	86	81	A	16.63	38	11	20	8	5.7	26	+136	+ 7	6.4	13.7	45	−0.16
7	Lilly Inds Inc Cl A	LI	86	81	A	18.88	4	20	25	10	22.6	254	+ 50	+ 89	9.4	19.4	19	−0.21
8	Praxair Inc	PX	84	77	C	46.00	4	23	24	13	155.7	3486	+ 35	+ 8	13.7	26.7	83	+0.82
9	Grace W R & Co	GRA	85	75	B	55.00	5	12	31	9	88.2	9863	+205	− 13	− 8.5	14.2	105	+1.76
10	Dexter Corp	DEX	85	70	B	30.75	4	16	373	13	23.7	513	+ 28	+ 1	7.3	11.4	58	+0.66

EXHIBIT 1-4.   Industry Group Focus.

profile has identified successful small and medium-size companies that have often been ignored by other publications, and it is recommended that the investor cut this section out for further study and reference.

FUNDAMENTALS OF CHART ANALYSIS

The two basic tenets of chart analysis—namely, trend identification and the principle of confirmation—which were both enunciated at the turn of this century, can be elegantly followed on the *Market Charts* page. A trend is a chart of the past that points to the direction in which something has been moving. For example, if the high and low prices for a day were to be higher than the high and low of the previous day, then the daily trend of these prices would be considered to be up; likewise, if today's price range was below yesterday's, the daily trend would be down. The determination of trends would be relatively academic except that they have generally carried a certain degree of intrinsic momentum. There has been nothing more true in the stock market than the fact that once price trends have been established, they are more likely to continue along the trend than to reverse themselves. A strong market today increases the likelihood of a strong market tomorrow.

A basic objective of stock market analysis is, therefore, to recognize the direction of the long-term trend and determine the probability of it not continuing. In the course of its existence, a trend will be beset by a number of corrections that are likely to threaten the trend's longevity. Prices on the markets, hence, seldom move straight up or down, but usually waver or react along the way, resulting in a series of waves within the prevailing trend. And the practical function of the market indexes shown on the *Market Charts* page is limited to a consideration of whether any given series of price movements is constituting a discernible trend and, if so, to what extent.[7] Indeed, it has been said that whoever knows what the market trend is, and when it is most likely to change, has all the knowledge necessary to make money in the markets.[8]

Trend-following systems work well as long as the market is in a definite trend pattern. However, the market also spends time in trendless patterns in order to prepare for a trend. The chart pattern of the Dow Jones Industrials identifies the continuation or reversal of the market trend, but whether this market action is bona fide and truly broad-based requires confirmation from the Dow Jones Transportation Average, shown on the *Market Charts* page as a smaller chart. The term *confirmation* is used to indicate that two market averages or indexes are moving in track. When two averages, or any two logically selected companion indicators, are not tracking each other, they are said to diverge. Divergences, therefore, are caused by a failure of the market to show confirmations.

The principle of confirmation guards against the error of drawing conclusions on the basis of movements of just one market average, and improves the reliability of a price forecast based on a chart signal. Since the Dow can be misleading, it is necessary to evaluate other market indexes and note the differences among them. The movement of one market average must be confirmed by another, related average; in fact, it has been said that all related averages or indexes should confirm before reliable inferences may be drawn. Conclusions based upon the actions of one average, unconfirmed by the others, are almost certain to prove misleading.

The concept of trend identification has been extended to the other indexes shown on the *Market Charts* page, and even to charts of industry groups and individual stocks. Investment decisions have been based on trends. When a major price uptrend has developed in an individual stock as evidenced by consistent daily or weekly price gains, a position should not be sold until the price action indicates that the basic trend has changed. Likewise, the principle of confirmation has been expanded to the broader market indicators, such as the NYSE advancing versus declining stocks line displayed here.

Two aspects of the price curves of market indexes and market sectors deserve attention when their very long-term patterns are compared with each other, or with those of other investment instruments such as bonds or precious metals.

First, stock market prices depicted on most charts do not incorporate returns from dividends, which can significantly augment total returns. A superior performance by the technology sector, for example, which offers little or no dividend income, could prove to be deceptive compared with the total return on the S&P 500 index after its average 5 percent annual dividend return has been factored in. The other adjustment arises from the long-term effects of inflation: All prices on stock and market charts are current prices, unadjusted for inflation. For example, when the Dow Jones Industrial Average stood close to 1000 in 1965, its inflation-adjusted value was about 300. When it dropped to a new low of 770 in 1982, its inflation-adjusted value was less than 85.[9]

HOW TO USE *INVESTOR'S BUSINESS DAILY* TO MONITOR THE MARKETS

The *Market Charts* page is devoted to a study of the markets, and gives a complete 7-month statistical snapshot of the stock market. The stock market, as a whole, represents a serious and well-considered effort on the part of well-informed people to adjust stock prices to such values as will exist, or are expected to exist, in the not too remote future. At any given time, there are numerous forces that are driving the stock market, such as corporate earnings, inflation, interest rates, and the fear and greed of the investing crowd. The final output resulting from all these driving forces is expressed in the stock market averages and indexes shown on the *Market Charts* page. And the best way to understand anything about stock market behavior is to sit in front of these market charts every day and really look at the market.

Charts of stock market averages are like fever charts, measuring the market's health. Since the market is not a single entity measurable by a single market average, the page shows large charts of the three major market indexes—namely, the Nasdaq Composite Index, the Standard & Poor 500 (S&P 500) Index, and the Dow Jones Industrial Average (DJIA)

(Exhibit 1-5a-c). The direction of the general market and, above all, whether the market has hit a top or has bottomed can be assessed by reviewing these charts simultaneously. They provide an overview of the health of the market as a whole from their daily price and volume behavior, and allow an understanding of their supply and demand dynamics during the prior day's trading—of where the money flowed during the previous day's activity—and an appreciation of overall market direction.

The charts are intentionally large and span a 7-month period. They are positioned exactly parallel to each other so that at important market tops and bottoms, confirmations or divergences (failures to confirm) between the Dow and the two other broader indexes can be recognized. Advances in the DJIA when confirmed by proportionate gains in the S&P 500 Index indicate a more universal advance, and one can be confident that the advance is likely to continue. Conversely, a decline of similar magnitude registered in both these stock indexes indicates that a downfall will more likely endure.

At other times, the DJIA may break below one of its earlier price support levels, whereas the broader S&P 500 Index may hold its own over the same period, thus signaling a divergence and indicating that the market may be stronger than suggested by the Dow. In general, more false signals have been noted with the Dow over the years than with the better-constructed market indexes such as the S&P 500 and the NYSE Composite Index.[10] In fact, when the DJIA has diverged from the S&P 500, the Dow has usually been the one proved to be wrong.

Changes in the closing value of the S&P Index have been compared with changes in the closing values of the Dow by dividing the S&P value into that of the DJIA. This figure is then multiplied by the change in the S&P to provide a value comparable to the movement of the Dow Industrials for the day. The market has been considered bullish when the S&P Index moves relatively higher than the DJIA, and bearish when it drops relatively lower than the Dow Industrials.

It is important to understand the messages contained in the Nasdaq chart. A rising relative strength line (Nasdaq

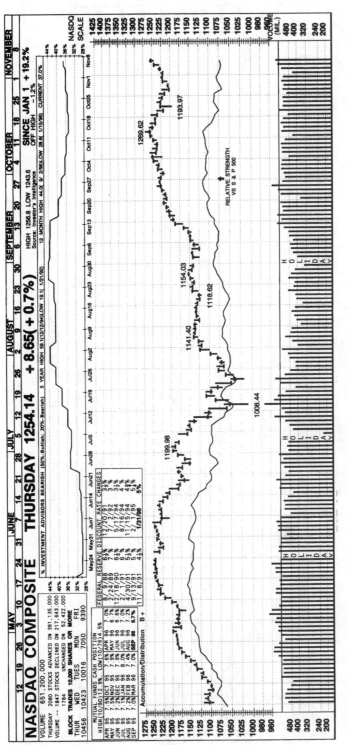

EXHIBIT 1-5a. Market Charts and General Market Indicators (Nasdaq Composite).

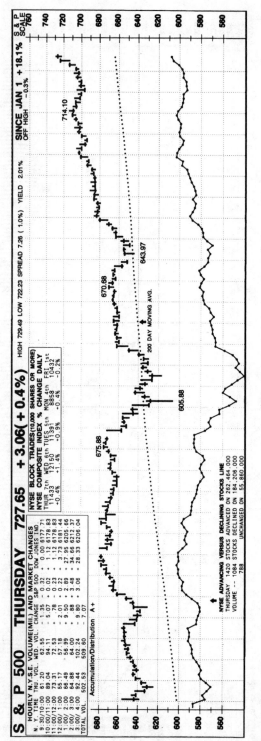

EXHIBIT 1-5b. Market Charts and General Market Indicators (S&P 500).

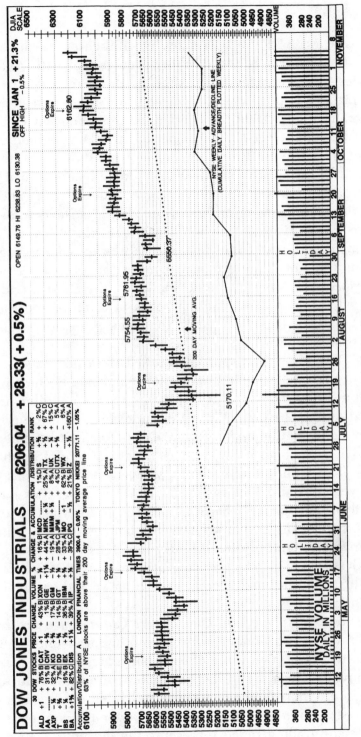

EXHIBIT 1-5c. Market Charts and General Market Indicators (Dow Jones Industrials).

Composite vs. S&P 500) is a bullish indicator because it reflects that, after a period of above-average fear with regard to riskier than average stocks such as those traded on the Nasdaq, there is now a sentiment of below-average fear. For example, in August 1994 the Nasdaq led the market by climbing 5.9 percent. Over the same period, the Dow gained 2.9 percent and the S&P 1.9 percent. A bullish sentiment expressed by the relative strength line should be confirmed by the Nasdaq Composite and other market indexes rising above their 200-day moving averages. Moreover, a Nasdaq trading volume exceeding NYSE volume (see item 9 in the *Psychological Market Indicators* on the *Market Charts* page) confirms that investors are acting more aggressively. When these aspects of Nasdaq trading shown on the chart are synchronized, it means that the market is in a bullish posture, and the path of least resistance for stock prices on a one-month basis is upward.

The Dow Jones Transportation and Utilities Averages are shown in the smaller charts on the left-hand side of the page. The *Dow Jones Transportation Average* (DJTA, called the Railroad Average before 1970) is the index on which the principles of confirmation and divergence of the market have been based. The *Dow Jones Utility Average* is composed of 15 public utilities. The Utilities have often preceded the Industrials in their reversal from a bear to a bull trend. Likewise, they have climbed proportionately higher than the Industrials or the Transports near the end of primary bull markets when institutional investors tend to direct money to defensive issues such as utilities. Divergence by the Dow Utilities from the course of the Industrials has had a good record as an indicator of a trend change.

The items displayed on the *Market Charts* page are *bar charts* drawn in two dimensions representing price and time[11] (Exhibit 1-6). The high value of each bar represents the maximum buying power, or bullish sentiment, expressed during that period, whereas the low value indicates the maximum bearish sentiment, or selling power, over the same time frame.[12] The trading range represents the dynamics between

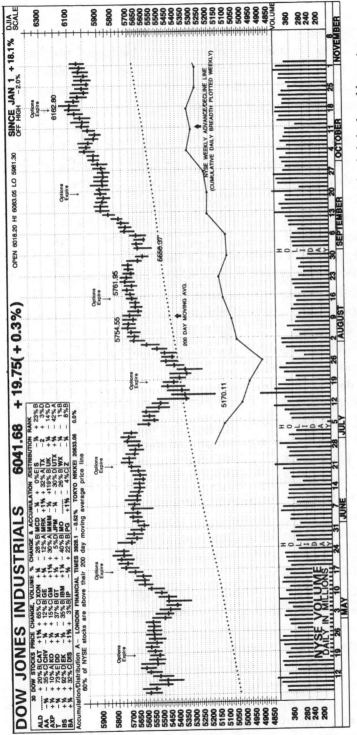

EXHIBIT 1-6. A Daily Bar Chart of the Dow Jones Industrial Average. Each vertical bar indicates the daily high and low prices, with the close price being shown by the horizontal crossline. Intermediate term trends, and support and resistance levels, can be drawn on the bar chart. The dotted line is the 200-day simple moving average of the Dow. Moving average crossover signals can be identified directly from the chart. The weekly NYSE Advance-Decline line is shown underneath the bar chart. Such a position allows divergences between the Dow and the A-D line to be identified directly from the chart. The proprietary Accumulation/Distribution rating of the Dow is shown below the box in the top left corner. The Daily NYSE trading volume is indicated as a vertical line arising from the bottom of the chart up to the level identified by the scale on the right.

23

buying and selling pressures. The process of drawing bars can be repeated for each trading day, and soon the highs and lows on the chart of an index (or stock) begin to produce patterns. A day in which the daily trading range is completely above, or below, the previous day's daily range without any overlap is called a *gap*. The number of shares traded on each day, or the volume of trade, is recorded on the bottom of the graph as a vertical bar extending up from zero to the correct figure in accordance with a scale along the side. Note that the market volume is always expressed as the number of shares traded on the NYSE, regardless of the market average to which it is being compared, which may be the DJIA or the S&P 500.

The *high*, *low*, and *close values* of each index, the percentage change from the previous trading day, and the overall performance (gain or loss) for the year (*since Jan 1*) are enumerated at the top of each chart (Exhibit 1-6). Locate these values on the charts.

There are some who believe that the last sale of the day reflects the nature of the trading activity for that day. Motion is the first rule of the market. There are usually many currents of movement during the hours of regular trading, but by and large there is usually one predominant, fairly general tide, be it ebb or flow. When one of these currents gets started, its own momentum carries it for some distance. It is natural, therefore, to assume that if the market has developed a definite current just before the close of one day, that tendency will continue into the next day's session.[13] The closing movements usually carry on in greater strength, and for a longer duration of time, than the movements which develop and pass during the course of a day's trading.

Another reason for the importance of closing prices is that the public, as it reads the record of the day's trading in the newspaper before the next day's opening, tends to judge the day as a whole and the prospects for the future largely by the closing prices, rather than by the conflicting price movements that prevailed during the whole day's trading.[14] Professional investors also watch the condition of the market throughout the day and respond to its changes, especially near the close of the market.[15] Thus, if prices close higher or lower, it implies that market professionals are bullish or bearish, respectively, for the day.[16] All these characteristics may no longer be the case because of the program trading, off-board trading, and block trading that represents market activity today, so that the last sale of the day now may well be the trade that just happens to occur at closing time.

Open value at the previous day's opening is shown only for the DJIA (Exhibit 1-6). The opening price reflects the overnight accumulation and balance of orders, usually by amateur traders. If there are more buyers than sellers, the averages invariably open higher. During bear markets, stocks have frequently opened strong and closed weak by the end of the day, whereas in bull markets, stocks open down but recoup and close up strongly. It has been argued that the best time to sell in the marketplace may be at the opening, whereby the market determines a fair opening price. If the opening is higher, the seller comes out ahead, while a lower opening confirms the stock's weakness and justifies its early sale.[17]

MARKET TRENDS

The bar charts show the price movements of the three major market averages. Prices move along the line of least resistance. They will go up if there is less resistance to an advance than to a decline, and vice versa. The direction of prices, and the speed of advance or decline, depends on the difference between the two resistances. Resistance has been measured by the volume of trading (number of shares traded) required to move prices by one point.[18]

In its simplest form, the theory holds that stocks will tend to trade, over a moderately short period of time, within a fairly narrow range of prices called a base wherein supply and demand are approximately equal. When demand increases, prices will break out of this trading range on the up side, and will make "new highs." As demand continues to grow, the price of the stock will rise to new levels which are higher than the previous high levels. When prices fall again during a correction, the price declines on the new move will not be as far down as they were the last time the stock declined. Thus, an uptrend exists when prices keep rising over time, with each price rally reaching a higher high value than the preceding rally, and each decline stopping at a higher level than the preceding decline.

Likewise, prices are declining over time in a downtrend when each decline falls to a lower value than the preceding fall, and each correction or rally stops at a lower level than the preceding rally. This makes it possible to draw "trend lines." In an uptrend, such a line encloses an upwardly sloping channel with all the highs within the top of the channel and all the lows within it down at the bottom.[19] Should upward price movements during an uptrend fail to penetrate the level of the last new high, and downward movements begin to move prices below the level of prices that marked the last low, then this uptrend pattern is considered reversed, and at least a temporary redirection of the trend channel may be expected.

The primary goal of any chart analysis is to recognize the direction of the long-term trend and to look for evidence that it is changing. Often the easiest way to identify a trend has been to inspect a chart visually and, in many cases, trends or their lack (trading ranges) become clearly visible. This is possible when a trend or a trading range is well in place. More commonly, trend followers use several charting techniques to detect a trend, and seek out confirmations of a signal from one indicator by other indicators before defining a trend.

THE MOVING-AVERAGE LINES

The commonest and oldest way to identify a trend has been through moving averages. The price and volume information that is displayed together on two of the large charts on the *Market Charts* page (Dow Industrials and the S&P 500) are shown with their *200-day moving averages* (Exhibit 1-6). Look at the dotted moving-average lines on these charts. The association of moving averages with market charts is unique to *Investor's Business Daily* and is not available in other financial newspapers. A moving average is a trend-following device whose purpose is to signal that an established trend has ended and a new one has begun. A moving average is a follower, not a leader, and its purpose is to track the progress of a trend.[20] Moving averages are the most widely used technique for market timing (technical analysis). The 200-day moving average of the DJIA is the most widely followed of all moving averages, and has been considered to be a reliable market timing indicator.

A moving average is simply an arithmetic average of successive numbers, such as the closing prices of a market average, over a specified period of time, such as 200 days. A 200-day simple moving average of the Dow can be constructed by adding the weekly closing prices of 30 consecutive Fridays, and dividing by 30. Every Friday thereafter, a new value is added and the one for 30 weeks earlier is dropped. This arithmetic average "moves" because the following week a new arithmetic average is calculated wherein the new closing price for that Friday is added on for the calculation, and the closing price 30 weeks earlier is removed. And so on for each new week. Thus the average is caused to "move" from week to week. The purpose of a moving average has been to smooth out daily price fluctuations so that a major trend of the market can be more clearly identified. A market's price position relative to its moving average serves to determine whether the market is responding to events or sentiments in such a way as to change its recent trend.

Buy or sell signals have been identified when the closing price of an index has been convincingly above or below its 200-day average.[21] Stocks should be sold when market prices are below the 200-day moving average *and* the moving-average line is itself sloping downward. Conversely, buying opportunities arise when the market is above its moving average *and* the moving-average line itself is rising. More specifically, when closing prices of the Dow move up from below the moving-average line, and cross the moving average after both have been declining for some time, a buy signal is generated. Confirmation of this initial buy signal occurs when the moving-average line itself changes course and turns up.[22] Likewise, when closing prices of the Dow move down from above the moving-average line, and cross the moving average after both have been advancing for some time, a sell signal is generated. Confirmation of this initial signal occurs when the moving-average line itself turns down.[23]

THE NYSE A-D LINE

Below the 200-day moving average line of the S&P 500 index is a line called the *NYSE Advancing vs. Declining Stocks* line (Exhibit 1-5). *Investor's Business Daily* is the only financial newspaper to display an advance-decline line every day for the NYSE.

The NYSE advance-decline line (A-D line) plots the difference between the number of NYSE stocks that are rising and the number that are falling. When a majority of the stocks are advancing, it means that there is more demand for stocks and a predominant buying power, and prices are likely to rise higher on that day. When more stocks are declining in price, the resulting increased supply of stocks and the greater selling pressures are likely to push prices even lower. In contrast to the DJIA, which represents only 30 stocks, the NYSE represents a broader market. The NYSE advance-decline line therefore measures, on a cumulative basis, the breadth of this market—it shows the action of all the stocks on the NYSE.

Generally, the NYSE A-D line will rise and fall in tandem with the DJIA line, indicating that the broad market, as represented by the NYSE, is confirming the message of the Dow. But when their paths diverge, it is a sign that the many small stocks that make up the broad market are weakening, and this weakness will eventually overtake the 30 large companies that make up the Dow. A reversal in the trend of the Dow Industrials and the entire stock market may be in the offing. The NYSE A-D line is able to pick up the first sign of problems.

Every day, the actual numbers of stocks on the NYSE that are advancing or declining in price, and those whose prices have remained unchanged, are also shown on the *Market Charts* page, just below the daily NYSE advance-decline line (Exhibit 1-5). These absolute numbers of advances and declines can be very helpful. Extreme numbers of advances or declines reflect marked buying or selling, and such extreme days have invariably heralded reversals of the market trend. More than 1000 advances or declines in a day, for example, has traditionally been the first indication of marked buying or selling, and extreme activity would be indicated on days when there are 1000 or more net advances less declines, or vice versa. When either or both conditions have been seen on 3 or more consecutive days, then a market top or bottom has been imminent.[24]

The cumulative daily breadth on the NYSE is summarized in a *weekly advance-decline line,* shown in the lowest big chart on the page, below the 200-day moving-average line of the Dow Industrials (Exhibit 1-6). This weekly indicator usually gives a more clear picture of the market's recent and current breadth and its trend. Trends between the daily and weekly advance-decline lines over the same period can, at times, be different because of the cumulative nature of the latter's construction. For example, a market that has been net or cumulatively up for the week will show an advancing weekly trend; however, that same week may have experienced 3 declining days so that the daily advance-decline line will be a declining one.

ACCUMULATION-DISTRIBUTION RATINGS

The action of the stock market is based on supply and demand and investor psychology. A good way to get a feel for the intermediate-term view of supply and demand is through the flow of funds—that is, by finding out where money is being invested. *Accumulation-distribution* ratings define the supply and demand pressures in the stock markets, and whether money is flowing into the market or out of it. The strength of the money flow on a particular day for a particular market index or stock has been estimated by multiplying the volume of shares traded by the average price. Average price is the sum of the high, low, and close prices, divided by three. Over any selected period of time, positive money flow would be the sum of the daily positive money flows accumulated during that period, whereas negative money flow, or the money distributed out, would be the sum of the daily negative money flows.

Accumulation of stocks by investors means that more cash is flowing into the market because of rising demand and more buying pressure, with the probability that the market indexes will rise higher. In this situation, component stocks in an index begin to trade upward on heavy volume or close at the high end of their daily price trading range.[25] Accumulation is usually initiated by knowledgeable market professionals who start buying at market lows when the unsophisticated are selling. Thus, on a price chart, a shift from distribution to accumulation creates a bottoming pattern. Conversely, the shift from accumulation to distribution forms a topping pattern.

During distribution, money is flowing out of the markets because of more selling than buying, leading to a greater supply of available shares. Component stocks of an index during distribution trade on heavy volume with declining prices, or close at the lower end of their daily trading range.[26] Market prices are likely to continue their decline during heavy distribution. Distribution is also occurring when the market is in an uptrend, or going sideways, and then shows heavy volume but no upward price progress, a phenomenon known as *churning*.[27] The explanation is that as more buying enters the market, it is met by an equal amount of selling. The usual result is a loss of upward momentum, and eventually an actual decline. When accumulation and distribution are equal, prices neither rise nor fall, but move sideways on a bar chart within a price range called a *consolidation* or *trading range*.

The accumulation-distribution ratings of the DJIA, S&P 500, and Nasdaq Composite are reported in the top left corners of their respective big charts (Exhibits 1-5 and 1-6). These proprietary ratings for the market indexes are unique to *Investor's Business Daily* and are not available in any other daily financial newspaper. The ratings are ranked from A to E, with A and B indicating accumulation, D and E describing distribution, and C being a neutral ranking when supply and demand pressures (i.e., selling and buying) are estimated as being roughly balanced.[28]

Hourly NYSE Trading Action

Price changes and volume percentage changes from the previous day's trading in each of the 30 Dow stocks are enumerated in a box at the top left-hand corner of the DJIA chart. *Hourly volume figures on the NYSE* are shown in a small box in the top left side of the S&P 500 chart, and these provide sensitive confirmations about potential turning points in the market. The table (Exhibit 1-5) shows the hourly market changes in the S&P 500 and the Dow. Here the hour-by-hour price changes, and hourly volumes, are compared with the same hours of the prior trading day. Such hourly movements become critical in detecting stock market tops when an initial market decline is taking place, or in identifying stock market bottoms when the first forces of strength are being mustered.[29] Some investors have been known to follow the hourly movements every day—to get under the very skin of, and have a real feel for, the daily market movements. The wide fluctuations in hourly trading necessitate the use of a one-day moving average.

Two periods of trading in the hourly trading box have traditionally been of significance. The first of these is the hour from 11 A.M. to noon.[30] Market professionals seem to make their moves each day after the first 90 minutes of trading, which are usually characterized by the execution of foreign orders and the trades made by the public. In fact, the first hour of trading is substantially influenced by what is happening in the futures and the bond markets, the European, especially the London, market, the "hot" news and rumors on earnings, and speculation on the 10 o'clock news announcements. The dust settles by 11 A.M., and it has been claimed that the trading characteristics during this hour have shown a good predictive correlation to the market 1 to 2 months hence. For example, a weakening in the 11 to 12 hour suggests that the overall market could be reaching a top. On the other hand, if the market has been trending lower, then a few days of strong 11- to 12-hour rallies may well be signaling that the market is bottoming and about to turn upward.

Similar correlations have been proposed for the last hour of trading but with predictions going 3 to 4 months out.

NYSE BLOCK TRADES

A box at the top of the large S&P 500 Index chart shows the daily *NYSE block trades* (Exhibit 1-5). Block trades are defined as trades of more than 10,000 shares on the NYSE. This information has been used to construct a *large block ratio* by dividing the volume of large block trades by the total volume on the NYSE.[31] Block trades reflect the sentiments of professional institutional investors, and they have been used to identify major reversal points in the stock market that take place when sustained buying or selling by the market professionals leads to overbought or oversold conditions.[32] A 5-week simple moving average has been used to smooth the fluctuations in the ratio. When the level of this moving average exceeds 50 percent (or 0.50), an overbought situation is usually present, signaling the time to sell. Conversely, an oversold condition is in effect when the moving average of the ratio falls below 20 percent (or 0.20).[33] Block trades on the Nasdaq are reported in a box on the top left corner of the large chart of the Nasdaq Composite.

MUTUAL FUNDS CASH POSITION

A data block at the top left corner of the large Nasdaq Composite Index chart presents a summary of the percentage *cash position of mutual funds* for each month. This is defined as the average percentage of cash, or cash equivalents such as money market instruments or short-term Treasury bills, held in the portfolios of stock mutual funds. Cash held by money market funds is not included because this money does not reflect the behavior of mutual fund managers controlling common-stock investments. The index is calculated by dividing the total amount of cash and cash equivalents held in equity mutual funds by the total amount of fund assets. Cash positions indicate how much buying power portfolio managers have in the market. It provides a measurement of the bullish or bearish sentiment of professional institutional investors such as mutual fund managers.

It has, however, become one of the inescapable truths of the market that the majority of market professionals do not beat the market. Year after year, more than 70 percent to 80 percent of professionally managed funds and portfolios have consistently failed to equal the performance of the S&P 500. One study undertaken by the Cowles Commission for Economic Research in 1933, and repeated in 1944, showed that the predictions of the nation's leading market managers hit the mark with 4 percent less accuracy than if their stock selections had been made completely at random.[34] Similar results were noted in another classic study of investment performance which examined the record of 115 mutual funds between 1955 and 1964.[35] The last decade has been no different. In 1994, for example, about 2800 stock mutual funds lost money, about 400 showed a gain, and only about 40 showed double-digit gains.

A cash reserve carries with it both the exemption from monetary loss and the inability to achieve profits. Prudent investment principles prescribe that when profit potential declines and risk levels rise, such as at stock market peaks, liquidation without concomitant purchases becomes necessary. The facts show otherwise, and most stock mutual funds have established a history of holding relatively small cash balances at stock market tops because of aggressive stock purchases at this inopportune time, thus increasing exposure to risk. Likewise, funds have adopted a misdirected defensive posture at the bottoms of market cycles. This inverse relationship over the last two decades between mutual fund cash positions and the market (the NYSE Composite Index) has dictated that mutual fund cash positions should be used as a contrarian indicator, whereby excessive sentiment by professional money managers on one side of the market can be expected to drive price moves in the opposite direction.

Historically, high cash levels of 12 percent or greater have occurred during the last months of bear markets and hence are a bullish signal. Conversely, cash levels of less than 9 percent have implied that the market may be near a significant peak, thus giving a bearish signal. Cash levels rise when fund managers are bearish and are selling stock to produce cash, or are unwilling to buy additional stocks. Some have explained that cash levels also rise when there is more new money deposited by investors. And the largest deposits of public dollars have come into funds at a time when public confidence in the ability to make money in the stock market has been at its height—namely, at the peak of long market rises. The low actual levels of cash at these times in the face of the large cash infusion underscores the bullish aggressiveness of fund managers at market tops. It reflects their misdirected concern that the holder of substantial amounts of cash may miss the potential profits generated from a hoped-for future market rise. In addition to equity fund cash positions, the absolute amount of cash deposited into various sectors of the market, such as aggressive growth funds or global funds, is of investment interest.

NOTES

1. Victor Sperendeo, *Trader Vic: Methods of a Wall Street Master* (John Wiley & Sons, NY, 1991).
2. Philip Fisher, *Common Stocks and Uncommon Profits* (PSR Publications, CA, 1984).
3. Robert Heilbroner, *The Making of Economic Society* (Prentice-Hall, Englewood Cliffs, NJ, 1962).
4. *Ibid.*
5. William O'Neil, *How to Make Money in Stocks* (McGraw-Hill, NY, 1991).
6. *Ibid.*
7. Raymond Righetti, *Stock Market Strategy for Consistent Profits* (Nelson-Hall, Chicago, 1980).
8. Sperendeo, *Trader Vic.*
9. Stephen Leeb, *Market Timing for the Nineties* (HarperBusiness, NY, 1993).
10. Robert Colby and Thomas Meyers, *The Encyclopedia of*

Technical Market Indicators (Dow Jones Irwin, Homewood, IL, 1988).

11. William Jiler, *How Charts Can Help You in the Stock Market* (Trendlines, NY, 1962). This paragraph was put together from Jiler's book.

12. Alexander Elder, *Trading for a Living* (John Wiley & Sons, NY, 1993).

13. Richard Schabacker, *Stock Market Theory and Practice* (B. C. Forbes, NY, 1930).

14. *Ibid.*

15. Elder, *Trading for a Living.*

16. *Ibid.*

17. Justin Mamis, with Robert Mamis, *When to Sell* (Simon & Schuster, NY, 1978).

18. Arthur Merrill, *Resistance: Technical Analysis of Stocks and Commodities,* Vol. 8, 1990, p. 112.

19. Sperendeo, *Trader Vic.* The best discussion on trendlines is presented in this book.

20. *Ibid.*

21. See the discussion on moving averages in Chapter 7: "The Internal Structure of Markets."

22. Gerald Appel, *Winning Market Systems* (Signalert Corp., Great Neck, NY, 1974).

23. *Ibid.*

24. Justin Mamis, *How to Buy* (Farrar Straus Giroux, NY, 1982). See also Gerald Appel, *Winning Market Systems,* and Martin Zweig, *Winning on Wall Street* (Warner Books, NY, 1990).

25. Investor's Business Daily, *Guide to High-Performance Investing* (O'Neil Data Systems, Inc., Los Angeles, 1993).

26. *Ibid.*

27. *Ibid.*

28. *Ibid.*

29. O'Neil, *How to Make Money in Stocks.*

30. Sam Weinstein, personal communication with *Investor's Business Daily.*

31. Colby and Meyers, *Encyclopedia of Technical Market Indicators.*

32. *Ibid.*

33. *Ibid.*

34. Richard Brealy, *An Introduction to Risk and Return from Common Stocks* (MIT Press, Cambridge, MA, 1982).

35. *Ibid.*

CHAPTER TWO

THE INTELLIGENT TABLES

SMART THINKING ON WINNING STOCKS

After a study of the market sector indexes, the industry groups, and the general market averages and indexes, one can now proceed to interrogate the performance of individual stocks. From the Contents, turn to the pages listed for the NYSE Tables, the Amex Tables, or the Nat. Mkts. Tables.

Stocks that have demonstrated unusually strong trading characteristics are identified every day in data blocks that are prominently positioned at the head of the stock tables. After the daily market averages, the most important indicator of the market trend is the behavior of those individual stocks that are leading the market. As long as the market's strongest stocks are continuing to perform well, the primary trend is considered to be in place and a bull market is in progress. A loss of market leadership characterized by a rising distribution (selling) of these stocks, or by a failure of winning stocks to follow through after a new breakout in price, is a most telling sign of a weakening market.[1]

It has been known for some time that in the analysis of the volume of shares traded, changes in volume relative to the recent past volume of trading have been more informative than the actual level of trading volume. Stock prices move in the direction of volume. Significant expansions and contractions in trading volume have invariably anticipated or helped confirm trends in market prices, and this observation forms the basis for the *volume percentage change* which is reported daily for every stock (Exhibit 2-3). It is different from the stan-

American Exchange

TOTAL VOLUME 21,121,890 CHANGE −10.3%

15 Stocks With Greatest % Rise In Volume

(Compared with last 50 days avg. volume. Stocks over $12 and ¼ pt change.)
Stocks up in price listed first. Stocks up with EPS & Relative Strength 80 or more are **boldfaced**.

EPS Rnk	Rel. Str.	Acc. Dis.	52-Week High	52-Week Low	Stock Name	Stock Symbol	Closing Price	Change	PE Ratio	Float (mil)	Volume (1000s)	Vol. % Change
64	55	B	18⅜	15⅛	Garan Incorporated	GAN	18	+ ¾	13	4.3	21	+621
3	5	E	60⅜	25	Cablevision System o	CVC	27	+ 1⅛	..	11	433	+485
75	63	A	14½	12	Cptl Reit Tax Exmpt	CRB	14½	+ ½	12	3.2	11	+470
1	43	D	16¼	9¼	Hngrn Tele & Cable	HTC	12	+ 1⅜	..	3.3	21	+294
99	72	B	23⅛	15⅛	Cubic Corp	CUB	21½	+ ⅜	20	5.3	17	+267
89	**91**	**B**	**48¼**	**18¼**	**Keane Inc o**	**KEA**	**49⅝**	**+ 3¼**	**37**	**11**	**122**	**+263**
88	**85**	**B**	**21⅞**	**10⅝**	**Watsco Inc Cl B**	**WSOB**	**20¼**	**+ 1¼**	**24**	**13**	**7**	**+250**
71	62	C	20½	16¾	Public Strg Prop Xi	PSM	20	+ ⅜	14	1.9	5	+221
47	86	B	14	7½	Far East Natl Bank	FEB	13½	+ ¼	15	3.2	4	+214
95	**94**	**A**	**15⅞**	**7¼**	**Selas Cp Of America**	**SLS**	**16¼**	**+ ¾**	**16**	**3.1**	**18**	**+168**
53	97	B	20⅞	4⅝	Golden Str Resource o	GSR	18½	+ ½	..	25	44	+147
75	92	A	12⅜	5⅞	Tubos Acero Mexico o	TAM	12⅝	+ ½	7	60	458	+147
99	65	E	20⅞	10⅜	Chad Therapeutics	CTU	16⅛	− ½	30	7.9	79	+273
46	16	E	19¾	9⅜	Sterling House	SGH	12	− ⅜	..	2.2	16	+204
58	98	A	35½	13¾	Bay Meadw/Cal Jk	CJ	34½	− ¼	31	4.8	97	+146

15 Most Active Stocks

EPS Rnk	Rel Str.	Acc. Dis	Stock Name	Closing Price	Chg	Vol. (mil)	Vol.% Chg
32	17	E	Trans World Airlines	8½	+ 1¼	4.07	+415
79	16	B	Ivax Corp	15⅞	+ ⅛	1.38	+87
1	**66**	**A**	**S & P Depository Rcpt**	**73 7/16**	**+ ⅜**	**1.36**	**+70**
16	11	E	Echo Bay Mines Ltd	7 13/16	+ 1/16	1.09	+116
32	30	B	Viacom Inc Cl B N V	36⅞	− ⅛	1.01	+6
27	**99**	**A**	**D I Industries Inc**	**2¾**	**+ ¼**	**0.77**	**+176**
51	22	C	U S Bioscience Inc	9 15/16	+ 3/16	0.62	+415
73	75	A	Hasbro Inc	42¼	+ ¼	0.59	+95
79	92	A	Cheyenne Software	30⅜	....	0.51	−45
1	2	D	Hearx Ltd	2⅛	....	0.48	+115
75	**92**	**A**	**Tubos Acero Mexico**	**12⅝**	**+ ½**	**0.46**	**+147**
3	5	E	Cablevision System	27	+ 1⅛	0.43	+485
9	73	A	Ampex Corp	7¼	− 5/16	0.32	−11
	45	B	First Austrl Prime Fd	8 13/16	+ 1/16	0.30	−5
	72	.	WEBS Canada	12¼	− ⅛	0.27	+1168

15 Most % Up

(Stocks Over $12)

EPS Rnk	Rel Str.	Stock Name	Closing Price	Net Up	Vol. (100s)	Vol.% Chg
1	43	Hngrn Tele & Cable	12	+ 1⅜	20,9	+294
94	94	Genrl Employment	12¾	+ 1¼	20,0	+50
46	57	Organogenesis Inc	19⅝	+ 1½	195,9	+101
75	**99**	**Saba Petroleum Inc**	**28¼**	**+ 1⅞**	**21,7**	**−5**
21	60	PLC Systems	22¾	+ 1½	120,9	−13
89	**91**	**Keane Inc**	**49⅝**	**+ 3¼**	**121,7**	**+263**
98	**99**	**Centennial Tech Inc**	**65⅝**	**+ 4¼**	**219,4**	**+110**
75	**99**	**U T I Energy Corp**	**23¾**	**+ 1½**	**19,4**	**+26**
88	85	Watsco Inc Cl B	20¼	+ 1¼	7,0	+250
98	95	Ballantyne of Omaha	16¾	+ 1	6,6	−50
7	19	Advanced Magnetcs	17	+ 1	16,9	+117
95	**94**	**Selas Cp Of America**	**16¼**	**+ ¾**	**17,7**	**+168**
3	5	Cablevision System	27	+ 1⅛	433,2	+485
64	55	Garan Incorporated	18	+ ¾	20,9	+621
75	**92**	**Tubos Acero Mexico**	**12⅝**	**+ ½**	**457,7**	**+147**

EXHIBIT 2-1. Proprietary Data Blocks that Screen the Stocks Showing the Strongest Current Price and Volume Activity.

dard volume measurement that gives the total number of shares bought and sold for the day. To determine volume percentage change, the normal trading level for every company is tracked during the prior 50 days, since each stock's average daily volume is different. The volume percentage change number shows each company's trading volume for that day in terms of its percentage change above, or below, its average daily volume of the last 50 trading days.[2] A figure of + 200 means that the stock traded on 200 percent more volume than normal.

The volume percentage change measurement identifies those stocks whose price changes are occurring on a greater than usual rise in volume. Since institutional investors account for the majority of trading volume for most equities, a heavier than average volume generally means that a directed effort is being made by knowledgeable investors or insiders to trade a stock. A major change in the trading volume of a stock has invariably been followed by a change in the trend of its price. In a bull market, winning stocks have risen on higher volume. Minimal price changes on heavy volume, a phenomenon known as *churning*, indicates that selling of the stock is just as heavy as its buying, and is often a sign that a price top may have been reached. Stocks that rise on low volume in a rising market should be avoided. Conversely, in a bear market, stocks falling on heavy volume have been the biggest losers. Sharply declining prices accompanied by a progressive contraction of volume usually indicates that selling is drying up and a bottom may have been reached.

Every day, the *Stocks with the Greatest % Rise in Volume* are highlighted in a data block at the beginning of the *Intelligent Tables* (Exhibit 2-1). Only those issues on the NYSE that are over $15 and have shown at least a 0.5 point change in price are considered, since the odds of success are relatively lower when investing in stocks below $10. On the American Exchange Prices tables, this screen is reduced to 15 stocks that are over $12 and have shown at least a 0.25 point change in price on abnormally heavy volume. In the Nasdaq News tables, the list is expanded to 100 stocks, but also limited to those stocks over $12 that have shown at least a three-eighths point change in price on unusually heavy volume.

Stocks that are up in price on abnormally heavy volume are listed first, and those with an EPS rank and relative strength rank of 80 or more are **boldfaced.** Stocks that have fallen in price on heavy volume are shown at the bottom of the data block. This list therefore allows a quick screening every day of all companies, regardless of size, where something unusual is happening. It is the best data block to begin a search for winning stocks every day. Those that are boldfaced, and whose prices have not already risen more than 10 percent above their most recent baseline, could represent investment opportunities worth monitoring closely. Here is a source for new and profitable investment ideas, because the appearance of a stock in this list has often prompted a buying opportunity, or alerted a selling signal. Check this block every day. At the end of each week, note those stocks that have appeared on successive days in this block, indicating that they have continued to rise in price, day after day, on strong volume. These few stocks deserve more study urgently.

Two other data boxes on the first page of the *Intelligent Tables* list the *Most Active Stocks* and the *Stocks Most % Up in Price* (Exhibit 2-1). With institutions such as mutual funds dominating market activity today, the *Most Active Stocks* reflect what institutional investors, such as mutual fund managers, are doing in the market. This box identifies whether institutional enthusiasm is leaning toward buying or selling and what the specific stock interests are. The most active stocks may represent fewer than 1 percent of the total number of issues traded but they can generate up to 20 percent or 25 percent of the total volume.[3] These lists have served to expose new industry groups that are coming in or getting out of favor, and to spot new profit opportunities and ideas. When two or three stocks of the same industry group have made the list for 3 weeks, it is a good indicator that this industry group is being most favored by the powerful market professionals. One or more of the "most actives" may be ready for a big move, and it may well behoove the investor to bring in all analytical skills to evaluate these industry groups and their individual issues. The quality of the stocks making the *Most Active* list can also give a clue to the overall market condition, and to where its substance or softness lies.[4] The presence of growth stocks on this list bodes well for the market; on the other hand, the appearance of the wrong types of stocks on this list, such as the defensive companies, could be an alarm that is worth heeding.

An additional piece of information that is not shown on this page but which needs to be examined daily together with the unique data blocks shown here are the number of new highs and new lows. These can be located from the Contents under *New Highs & Lows* (Exhibit 2-2). Every business day, some stocks close at higher or lower prices than they have during the preceding 52 weeks, and these stocks are listed in the New Highs and Lows table. Note that the reference frame for defining new highs and lows is not the current calendar year but the preceding 52 weeks.

This data block is one of the most important and valuable for prospective investment profits. Companies making new highs invariably move even higher. Stocks that have doubled in price are more likely to double again than any other ascertainable group. Conversely, companies whose prices have fallen over 90 percent, especially to a level below a dollar, continue to underperform. There is a strong economic reason that a price makes a new high or a new low for the year, and in many cases there is something significant happening in the company. The act itself indicates a fundamental background change, and even though the reasons may not yet be clear, they are clearly of sufficient force to result in a new price record.

Every corporation has within it a certain number of strengths and weakness, and a certain number of neutrals that can turn into additional strengths. A new price high identifies a company with the greatest number of strengths. The chronology of the move is especially important: There is much more potential strength in a new high made early in a price move than in a new high in which a price rise has been developing over many weeks. A chart review would clarify the freshness of the present move. Hence, when stocks make their

328 New Price Highs

NYSE (n) – 186 New Highs, 25 New Lows
NASDAQ – 117 New Highs, 60 New Lows
AMEX (a) – 25 New Highs, 5 New Lows

Stocks listed within each group,
are in order of greatest increase in volume.
Closing price and EPS Rank are also shown.

(NASDAQ NMS common stocks over $2 only)

†See Graphs in NYSE, NASDAQ or AMEX "Stocks In The News"

Name & Exchange		Close	EPS	Name & Exchange		Close	EPS
FINANCE (93)				LehmnBrHdg (n)	LEH	28	58
FranklinRes (n)	BEN	71½	85	Sunamerica (n)	SAI	42	96
RockfordInds	ROCF	22⅝	98	FedHmLnMtg (n)	FRE	104⅞	84
FirstAllianc	FACO	30¼	84	ConcrdEFS	CEFT	30	96 †
WEBS NthInd (a)	EWN	18⅝	..	Central Secur (a)	CET	25¼	.. †
FirstUnion RE (n)	FUR	8⅝	45	PrefrdIncFd (n)	PFD	15	..
RgncyRealty (n)	REG	24½	80 †	SoeastnThrf	STBF	15½	..
EqtyRsdntl (n)	EQR	39⅛	92 †	HousehldInt (n)	HI	91⅞	80
UrbnShpCntr (n)	URB	27¼	78	AvalonPpties (n)	AVN	26	18
SntAnitaRlty (n)	SAR	25⅜	30	SallieMae (n)	SLM	90	86 †
DevDvsfd (n)	DDV	34½	83	InterRegion (n)	IFG	35	78 †
InnkprUSA (n)	KPA	12⅛	90 †	DukeRealty (n)	DRE	36	66
FelCorStes (n)	FCH	35⅜	15	MBNA (n)	KRB	39⅞	92
GenAmInvstr (n)	GAM	23⅝	..	CapsteadMtg (n)	CMO	22⅝	85 †
MoneyStore	MONE	19⅝	96 †	BradleyRE (n)	BTR	17	96
VornadoRlty (n)	VNO	4⅞	81	HlthRetir (n)	HRP	18½	52
FirstIberianF (a)	IBF	9½	.. †	LeggMason (n)	LM	37	70
Counsllr Tan (n)	CTF	19⅜	..	CBL Assoc (n)	CBL	24⅜	96
FirstFinlFund (n)	FF	15¾	..	CB Germany (n)	GXG	37¼	..
SalmBrosFd (n)	SBF	16⅝	..	WEBS Spain (a)	EWP	15½	..
Gemini II Cap (n)	GMI	28	..	QstValue Cap (n)	KFV	38	..
ConsumerPrt	CPSS	14¼	9.	MackenFncl	MKFCF	13¼	81
SPDepRecpt (a)	SPY	73⅞	1 †	**BANKS (52)**			
Hlth Cre Ppty (n)	HCP	37½	59	Citfed Bncp	CTZN	48¾	89
SirromCap	SROM	38	88	Sandwich Bk	SWCB	28¾	90
DeanWiDisc (n)	DWD	63½	78	CentryBncrp	CNBKA	14¼	87 †

EXHIBIT 2-2. An Example of the New Highs and Lows List.

debut on this list, their day's trading should be examined. If the new high was made, for example, by an eighth of a point and the stock closed lower for the day, then the stock may well have reached its top, and the current rally in its price leading to the new high value would most likely exhaust itself soon.[5] On the other hand, a stock that appears on the new highs list for the first time and trades up a couple of points on heavy volume is more likely to be set for a genuine break upward.[6]

This list, as presented in *Investor's Business Daily,* is more instructive than the high-low lists found in other financial newspapers because it is the only one organized by broad industry groups. Those industries showing the most stocks making new highs are given first. The industry group with the greatest number of stocks making new highs is **bold-faced**, as is the number of stocks in that group. Furthermore, a plus sign (+) to the right of the EPS rank of a stock in this chart indicates that a graphic portrait of the stock can be found in the *Stocks in the News* chart gallery. The *New Highs* table therefore provides a superb screen for identifying group leadership and those winning stocks that are currently setting the pace in the market. On the other hand, the *New Lows* table boldfaces the industry groups with stocks showing the largest number of new lows and their actual number. When there are more new highs than new lows, the market is advancing, while a declining market will show more new lows than new highs.

A moving average of the net difference between the daily new highs and new lows has been of value as the stock market bottoms. A shrinking number of net lows would indicate more resistance to decline. Internal market strength or deterioration invariably shows up in the new highs and new lows values before the values of the market averages change direction, and before market averages cross their 200-day moving average lines.[7] A consistent and reliable sign of market divergence has been a new high in a market average associated with fewer new 52-week highs, thus indicating weakness in the broad market and an impending correction.[8]

Just tracking the absolute number of new 52-week highs can also be of value. In 1987, for example, when the DJIA hit its own new high of 2338 in February, the number of 52-week new highs was 258. The Dow reached a further record in April at 2406, but this was associated with only 130 new highs, and the erosion continued when the market hit a top of 2722 with only 137 new highs.[9] The deteriorating enthusiasm in a soaring market was obvious. A very small number of 52-week new highs suggests a market or cycle bottom, especially if the number of new lows is very high.

THE INTELLIGENT TABLES

A superior portfolio of common stocks can be put together and their performance tracked with unrivaled thoroughness using the proprietary *Intelligent Tables*, so called because vital information which is necessary for smart investing is found exclusively in these tables. Modern computer programming technology has allowed *Investor's Business Daily* to completely redesign its newspaper stock tables so that powerful statistics, available at one time only to institutional investors, are now published daily for the ordinary person in the *Intelligent Tables*. These proprietary statistics cannot be found in any other daily financial newspaper. Taken together, they provide the individual investor with a formidable arsenal to develop or adopt winning investment systems.

In each of the NYSE, Amex, and Nasdaq sections, the tables follow a similar format. Stocks that have made new highs in their price and/or were up a point or more in price during the previous day's trading are **boldfaced,** whereas those that made new price lows or were down a point or more in price are <u>underlined</u>. Boldfaced stocks that are making all-time highs are a unique group because they possess the property of no overhead resistance. Being at an all-time high price means that there is no one holding the stock at a higher price. In other words, there are no potential sellers who are looking to break even after having bought the stock at a higher price. Boldfacing of stocks that are up one or more points highlights issues that have made a significant move for the day, and are therefore deserving of greater inspection.

This technique of boldfacing or underlining not only highlights desirable or unfavorable stocks, but also gives the overall tables a certain look.[10] A rising market should normally show more new highs and fewer new lows, so that the tables will have a lot of boldfacing when the market is strong. Conversely, a declining market is often associated with a rising number of new lows and fewer new highs, so that when the market is weak, there is a lack of boldfacing. In a bear market, most stocks would be underlined. Hence, the general health of the market may be diagnosed just by stepping back and looking at the general appearance of the tables in terms of boldfacing or underlining.[11]

HOW TO USE *INVESTOR'S BUSINESS DAILY* TO MONITOR INDIVIDUAL STOCK PERFORMANCE

The first page of the *NYSE Intelligent Tables* has a box entitled *How to Read Our Intelligent Tables*. This must be read first, just like the directions that are first read for any new product that is bought. Every day, the tables show routine data such as the stock symbol, the high, low, and closing price of each stock during the previous day's trading, the high and low prices over the previous 52 weeks of trading, and the trading volume or number of shares that were bought and sold on the previous business day (Exhibit 2-3). The 52-week High Low column shows the highest and lowest trading price of the stock during the last 52 weeks. The letters NH or NL in place of an actual price quotation indicates that a new price high or a new price low occurred during the reported day of trading. The 52-week high price is **boldfaced** if the closing price of a stock on the reported trading day is within 10 percent of a new high in price. Other standard data such as the price/earnings ratio and the dividend yield (*% Yld*) are shown only on certain days each week.

EPS	Rel Str	Acc. Dis.	% Ann Ern. Gro.	Qtr EPS % Chg	Qtr Sales % Chg	Next Qtr Est.	% yld	Stock & Symbol		Closing Price	Chg.	Vol.% Chg.	Vol. 100s	Float (mil)	52-Week High	52-Week Low	Day's Price High	Day's Price Low	# of Funds Own
3	40	B	...	...	−26↓	.....	..	Metricom Inc	MCOM	14¼	−½	−77	315	10	20½	9¼	15	14⅛	17↓o
96	1	.	+37	+999↑	+276↑	.....	..	MetrisCos	MTRS	22¼	−1¼	−73	1243	2.4	25¾	20⅛	24	21¾	...
1	**75**	**.**	...	...	...	.....	..	**MetroNtwks**	**MTNT**	**23¼**	**+1¼**	**−86**	**802**	...	**N H**	**19⅛**	**23¾**	**22½**	... k
75	51	B	...	...	+27↓	0.10	..	MetroOneTel	MTON	10½	+⅛	+22	1269	6.3	16¼	8⅝	10¾	10⅜	...
1	2	D	...	...	+31↑	.....	..	Metrocall	MCLL	5⅝	+⅛	+7	1145	5.9	26¼	5⅛	5¾	5½	27↑o
67	77	C	...	+133↑	+19↑	.....	..	Metrologic	MTLG	13½	....	−92	6	1.6	16¾	8¾	13½	13½	5
63	77	B	+7	+6↓	+2↓	0.34	..	MetropolBnc	MSEA	17 15/16	+ 3/16	+51	151	2.5	18¼	12	18	17¾	6↑
34	**1**	**.**	**+8**	...	**+27↑**	.....	..	**MtrFncl**	**METF**	**11½**	**+¾**	**−10**	**168**	**3.5**	**N H**		**11½**	**10½**	...
89	86	B	+20	+42↑	+28↑	0.29	..	Metrotrans	MTRN	14½	....	−68	14	1.6	15¼	7	14½	14½	2↑
22	29	B	...	...	+94↑	.....	..	Metrowerks	MTWKF	10	+⅛	−13	20	11	15¾	8¼	10	9 11/16	6
47	63	A	...	+9↓	+9↑	.....	2.3	MetroWstBk	MWBX	4⅜	+ 1/16	−87	20	8.9	4½	3½	4⅜	4⅜	3
75	89	.	...	+100↓	+52↓	.....	..	MetzlerGp	METZ	25	−⅝	−91	220	...	25¾	19½	25¾	25	...
25	3	E	...	0	+12↑	.....	..	MiamiSubs	SUBS	⅝	+ 1/32	+73	1224	5.9	2¼	½	11/16	9/16	2
6	74	B	...	−68↓	+17↑	0.19	1.6	MichaelFood	MIKL	12½	+⅛	−95	22	11	13½	9½	12½	12⅜	28↓

EXHIBIT 2-3. The Proprietary Intelligent Tables (Nasdaq Stocks).

EARNINGS PER SHARE (EPS) RANKINGS

Earnings power and earnings growth are the most important fundamental determinants of a company's financial success and the price of its stock. Traditionally, a simple ratio of a stock's current reported four quarters earnings per share versus the reported earnings for four quarters one quarter earlier has been a sound basis to rank stocks for their relative earnings growth. Stocks scoring high in this ranking have invariably shown a high correlation to positive price performance 6 months later.

A study by William O'Neil & Co., a sister company of *Investor's Business Daily Inc.*, has shown that the greatest stocks of the last 40 years have uniformly had strong earnings growth as their one common characteristic for success that far outweighed any other.[12] The rate of earnings growth (i.e., acceleration in earnings) had even stronger associations with winning stocks. Earnings growth must be sustained over the past 5 years, and must still be in progress, extending to the most recent two quarters. Stocks that are leading the market have shown an annual compounded growth rate in earnings of 25 percent to 50 percent per year or even more, with earnings in the most recent quarters being 25 percent to 30 percent higher than in the same quarters of the year before.

These vital characteristics of earnings strength are measured in a unique proprietary statistic called the *earnings per share* (EPS) rank, which is reported every day, for every stock, only in the *Intelligent Tables* (Exhibit 2-3).[13] EPS measures a company's earnings growth over the past 5 years and the stability of that growth. Then, the percentage change in the earnings of the last 2 quarters versus the same quarters a year earlier is combined, and averaged with the 5-year figure. The result is now compared with every stock listed (more than 6000) in all the stock tables (NYSE, Amex, and Nasdaq OTC) and ranked on a scale of 1 to 99, with 99 being the highest. An EPS rank of 85 means that a company's audited earnings ranked in the top 85 percent of the more than 6000 companies being measured. The EPS rank gives each stock an objective relative measurement of reported earnings. Strong companies have an EPS of at least 80, and market leaders have had an EPS of 95 and higher.

RELATIVE STRENGTH (REL.ST.) RANKINGS

An obvious method of evaluating the overall performance of a stock is to compare the stock's performance with that of the overall market. By comparing the percentage change in the price of a stock with the percentage change in the price of an unmanaged market index, one can establish whether the stock is performing better or worse than the market.[14] This is one way to tell when the majority of investors have the same level of confidence for a company's prospects. The price performance of a company's stock is the parameter that reflects objectively the market's appraisal of that company. This characteristic is measured by another proprietary statistic called the relative strength (Rel.St.) rank number, which is also reported for every stock, each day, only in the *Intelligent Tables* (Exhibit 2-3).

The relative strength rank number is a comparative time-weighted indicator that compares the percentage change of a stock's price over the past 12 months with the change in price of every other stock listed on the exchanges. The results are ranked on a scale from 1 to 99.[15] A relative strength of 99, the highest possible, means that a stock's price gain has outperformed 99 percent of all other stocks in the past 12 months. A relative strength of 57 indicates that this stock outperformed 57 percent of all other stocks in the entire marketplace. Here is an objective way of measuring the market valuation or price performance of any stock, or even an industry group, against all others.

On the basis of empirical testing, some have proposed a time period of 26 weeks for the determination of relative strength.[16] In this measure, the ratio of the current price to the 26-week moving average of the stock is used. The closing price of the stock on Thursdays is used as the current price, and for the calculation of the moving average. This ratio is compared with the same calculation for all the other stocks in the database that is being followed. The stocks are then ranked on the basis of this ratio, and the top 10 percent are then investigated for their investment merits. This method is very time-sensitive, since the current price of each stock is compared with its own moving average. The ratio can drop quickly, giving an early warning of a change in trend for that stock.

The power of relative strength ranking lies in its cross-sectional analysis, a comparative approach whereby each stock is evaluated relative to all the others. A rising relative strength does not always mean that the absolute or actual price of the stock is appreciating, but only that it is outperforming the market. In a declining market, for example, if the price of a stock fell less than the overall market decline, it would show a high relative strength. In this case, both the stock and the market are losers, but the stock's loss is relatively less than that of the market. If the market was simply moving sideways, but a stock was showing improving relative strength, then that stock would be on its way up. Thus, the relative strength number does not assess each stock in isolation to determine individual returns or outcomes, nor does it rely on predictions, projections, or forecasts. It simply ranks the stocks on the basis of their price performances.

It has also been shown that if a stock performed consistently better or worse than a market over a few swings, then that relative strength or weakness would very likely continue.[17] Groups of stocks in strong relative strength uptrends are likely to continue to outperform the market until relative strength loses momentum and changes direction on a major trend basis.[18] This generally takes many months to develop. Conversely, stocks in major negative relative strength trends can underperform the broad market for a very long time. Hence, the idea of relative strength simply dictates that stocks that have done comparatively well in one period are expected to do comparatively well in the next. Earnings momentum (EPS rankings) and relative strength are invariably interrelated: Earnings, or the perception of rising earnings, drive stock prices, and stocks at the top of the relative strength list are usually the ones whose earnings estimates have been repetitively raised by analysts. The combination of high relative strength and high EPS rankings from the *Intelligent Tables* has been a simple yet unsurpassed screening method for picking strong stocks.

William O'Neil & Co. has also shown that the best-performing stocks of the last 40 years had an average relative strength of 87 *before* their major price upturns began.[19] Stocks with high relative strengths are the strongest stocks in the market and are the market leaders which move more quickly on the upside than most other issues. They are the best buys during a market uptrend, and they make new highs on days when the market averages are making new highs.[20] Some have recommended that such stocks should be purchased when they have made new price highs, whereas others have found it more profitable to buy them during reactions, or sellouts, because the chances of faster returns have been better.

High relative strength and an annual earnings growth rate of 20 percent or better in the face of an adverse economic environment are a particularly strong testament to a company's leading role in the products or services provided. The results of investing in such companies have been outstanding. In 1991, top-ranked growth-stock mutual funds that invested in such issues were up as much as 96 percent, and top-ranked money managers were up better than 100 percent. On the other hand, it has been cautioned that relative strength value may not be the best way to monitor a stock for a possible sale when it is bucking the market's downtrend, because relative strength is invariably a lagging indicator in this situation. A stock may decline substantially in price before its proprietary relative strength value shows a drop because of the way the relative strength calculation is weighted.[21] Instead, a decline in the accumulation-distribution rankings in the *Intelligent Tables* by two grade rankings—from A to C, for example—is a better indicator to time the sale (see later in this chapter).

Relative strength should not be the impetus for investment decisions, but rather should serve as a confirmation or warning tool in confirming good opportunities or flagging potential pitfalls. For example, if a stock price is below its moving average, it may well be prudent to let the issue pass despite a high relative strength. Divergences between earnings momentum and relative strength have been important; relative strength has been especially vital when a company has looked extremely strong in terms of its earnings power and stability but weak in its relative strength, or when a stock price has moved higher but its performance relative to the rest of the market has been weak.

An appreciation of relative strength leads logically to the following investment strategy.[22] Start with those industry groups which show the best relative strength, preferably groups which are in the act of definitely turning up after a long decline in their relative strength. Pick the stocks with the best relative strengths within the strong relative strength industries. Then identify the stocks with the best chart patterns from the strong relative strength stocks. These final choices can be expected to outperform during most market movements. They should be sold when they stop outperforming, as indicated by declines in their relative strength, or when the general market milieu becomes unfavorable for stock investment.

VOLUME PERCENTAGE CHANGE

This unique parameter has been discussed earlier. It is calculated and listed every day for every stock in the *Intelligent Tables*.

ACCUMULATION-DISTRIBUTION RATINGS

The supply and demand for a stock during the prior 40 days of trading are identified by the proprietary *accumulation-distribution* ratings (Acc.-Dis.) found in the Intelligent Tables. Accumulation (more buying than selling) occurs when a stock's price rises on heavy volume or its price closes at the high end of its daily trading range.[23] There is demand for the stock, and this raises the probability that its price will rise higher. Conversely, a stock is regarded as undergoing distribution (more selling than buying) when it drops in price on heavy volume, or closes at the lower end of its daily range.[24] Distribution is invariably followed by further price declines.

The Acc.-Dis. parameter is calculated by multiplying the percentage change in a stock's daily price by its volume. The result is either added to or subtracted from a cumulative total, depending on whether the prices have risen or fallen from the day before.[25] An A or B rating means that a stock is showing accumulation—that is, there has been more buying than selling of the stock during the prior 40 trading days and people have been accumulating the stock by buying it. Money is flowing into the stock. C is a neutral rating, and a D or E means that there has been more selling than buying, with a stock being distributed out from investment portfolios. The flow of money is out of the stock. The daily rank (A to E) is further adjusted for the percentage change in the close price relative to the stock's daily trading range. Any unusual spikes in volume are eliminated to smooth out the data.

When stock prices are consolidating as a base, or the price is beginning to break out of a base, the stocks should have an Acc.-Dis. ranking of A or B.[26] After a move up, a stock that goes into a base formation should maintain at least a C rating.[27] It is time to sell if a stock's rating has fallen to D or E, since lower prices invariably follow. An industry group, or the general market, is showing weakness when the winning stocks with high rankings in that industry or market index are falling down to rankings below C.[28]

INSTITUTIONAL SPONSORSHIP

Few winning stocks are so friendless as to be without a sponsor. Institutions (mutual funds, pension funds, insurance companies, bank trust departments, and charitable institutions) account for the majority of all trading today. Institutional money managers are the main movers of stock prices, and leading stocks usually have institutional backing.

Institutions spend considerable time and money in researching a company, and are therefore in close touch with the company's progress and are presumably in a favored position to know its real worth. Institutional sponsorship hence provides independent confirmation of the appropriateness of an individual investor's stock selection. A company should still be considered undiscovered, and therefore having the potential for further significant price rises, if institutional ownership is less than 5 percent to 8 percent. On the other hand, a stock has probably seen its maximal initial price rise when institutional holdings exceed 15 percent. Large institutional holdings can also make a stock very volatile on the downside: A disappointing earnings quarter can lead to simultaneous selling by institutions with precipitous declines in stock prices. Sponsorship thus gives rise to support levels on declines, and resistance levels on advances.

In addition to the extent of institutional backing, the quality of this support is critical. More than 80 percent of all institutional money managers underperform the stock market so that it becomes vital to know whether the stock is being backed by the top-performing managers. The proprietary *institutional sponsorship rankings* reported weekly in the *Intelligent Tables* analyze the *quality* of each stock's institutional backing. Only mutual funds are used in this assessment of the quality of institutional sponsorship because their managers are the most aggressive traders. The 3-year performance of all mutual funds owning the stock is averaged and ranked from A, for the best performance, to E for the worst. If a top-performing mutual fund owns a stock, that stock has a greater likelihood of being a winner. Getting to know the investment philosophies and characteristics of certain top-performing mutual funds can be an additional asset.

MANAGEMENT PERCENTAGE OWNERSHIP

The *management percentage ownership* (*Mgmt % Own*), reported weekly in the *Intelligent Tables*, is the percentage of stock held by the officers and directors of a company, and is based on information provided in company documents filed each year. Only top management with broad decision-making power is included in this measurement.[29] The percentage of stock held by management is calculated by dividing stock held by management by total shares outstanding. Those companies for which there is no management ownership, or no information is available, are marked by ellipses (...).

Studies have shown that stocks tend to perform better when management holds a sizable investment in the company. A high financial stake in the company's welfare tends to make management's interests the same as that of its shareholders, with a particular eye on the stock price. Many investors also feel more confident when there is a personal financial participation and commitment by management to the company's products and services. This parameter has also helped identify emerging growth stocks such as the biotechnology firms which, in the earlier stages of their growth cycle, have a higher percentage of management ownership. About 15 percent to 20 percent is considered good ownership, although big-capitalization stocks will expectedly show a lower percentage ownership by management. Anything over 30 percent is excessive and carries the problem of volatile price declines when management decides to liquidate. Stocks with a high concentration of management ownership by a few insiders should be avoided.

Management ownership, however, does not guarantee a winning performance, and many winning stocks have not had much management ownership. The management's holdings figures are different from, and do not reflect, insider trading. Insider buying is a good indication that a company's business prospects are good, since presumably knowledgeable people are putting their own money on the line. But insider selling has not shown a good correlation, since top managers could sell for personal reasons or to diversify their holdings.

INDUSTRY GROUP STRENGTH

Stocks in strong-performing industry groups do better than those in weaker groups. The proprietary 6-month relative strength ranking of each stock's industry group allows the strength of each stock to be valued in the context of its *industry group strength*, which is displayed every week. An A ranks the industry group's performance in the top 20 percent of all 197 industry groups, and an E puts it in the bottom 20 percent.

HOW TO USE *INVESTOR'S BUSINESS DAILY* TO FURTHER MONITOR NASDAQ STOCKS

Investor's Business Daily believes that the Nasdaq market is the home of the exciting, young companies that are emerging as the new market leaders. Hence the *Intelligent Tables* covering the Nasdaq stocks report additional proprietary statistics to give the individual investor a winning investment advantage. These statistics are not found in any other daily newspaper. Reading from left to right in the tables, this additional information on Nasdaq stocks includes fundamental statistics on earnings, sales, P/E ratios and dividend yields, and ROE (Exhibit 2-3).

Earnings are the fuel that propels the U.S. stock market, and American companies have learned to focus relentlessly on earnings and react swiftly to market shifts. Every corporation strives to keep its annual and quarterly earnings up, or else its share price goes down as investors bail out. The *percentage annual earnings growth* is a figure that measures a company's earnings growth rate over the past 3 to 5 years. If a company has not been in business for at least 3 years, no figure is given. The *percentage quarter EPS* shows the percentage change in quarterly earnings relative to the comparable quarter of the previous year. To put the number in better perspective, an up or down arrow shows whether the EPS growth is higher or lower than the prior period. No figure is given if a company reported a loss in its most recent quarter, compared with either a profit or a loss a year earlier.

In contrast to records of past earnings, projected earnings estimates are opinions, but gain importance as numerical views of expectations, and changing expectations have influenced stock prices. Most investment institutions have analysts who produce earnings forecasts for the companies that they follow. The *annual earnings estimate*, which is reported three times each week, is based on the consensus earnings estimates that are assembled in the large proprietary *Investor's Business Daily* database. If a company is not followed by analysts, or no analysts' reports have been collected, then no figure is provided. A *quarterly earnings estimate*, based on recent analysts' reports, is reported twice each week.

Rising sales volume is the sine qua non for expanding profits in most growth companies. A sale is the single most important basic activity of any business, and it has been proposed that any study of a corporation should logically begin with an examination of the stability and rates of growth of its sales.[30] Without sales, business survival is impossible. A *percentage quarterly sales* figure shows the percentage change in quarterly sales relative to the comparable quarter from a year earlier. To put the number in better perspective, an up or down arrow is used to indicate whether the sales growth rate is higher or lower than the prior period. No figure is given for most banks and other financial institutions, which often release only a limited quarterly statement.

The *P/E ratio* was born out of a premise that price is driven by earnings. When trailing (the past 4 quarters or past 12 months) earnings are used, the ratio is called a trailing P/E ratio, and this has been the conventional method for stock valuation. Many growth-stock investors are not interested in trailing earnings, although trailing earnings showing several quarters of accelerated profits have helped identify companies that are on a steady growth path. More commonly, investors have preferred to look ahead rather than behind, and forecasts made of future earnings are being used to determine the P/E ratio, which is then called a forward-looking P/E ratio. Both aspects of the P/E ratio are addressed in the *Intelligent Tables* for the Nasdaq stocks. Once a week, the table shows a company's *P/E ratio on estimate*, based on analysts' estimates for the *following* year. If a company is losing money, then no ratio is reported. On the other hand, P/E ratios based on trailing 12-month earnings are displayed on 2 days each week.

A very large number of outstanding shares requires a greater volume of buying to raise the price because of the large supply of stock available. The more widely owned a stock and the larger its institutional following, the more likely that everything known about the stock is reflected in its price. On the other hand, market inefficiencies that lead to large profits are more likely to be realized with the smaller and less analyzed companies. Average returns on stocks with low market capitalization have been shown to be triple those of the largest companies. The number of shares available for trading or a stock's supply—that is, a company's outstanding stock minus shares owned by management—is listed every day for the Nasdaq stocks as *shares float*.

In addition, the last column of the Nasdaq tables shows the following information on a rotational weekly basis:

1. *Percentage stock held by management.*
2. Number of mutual *funds that hold the stock.*
3. *Percentage price above/below 10-week average price.* This figure shows where the stock is relative to its average price during the past 50 trading days. It is often significant when a stock that has been trading above its moving average falls below it, and vice versa.
4. *Return on equity.* This figure is calculated by dividing the average common stock equity in the past 2 years by net income for the most recent year. ROE tells investors how effectively their money is being used by the company. Some have called it the single most important fundamental characteristic of a company.
5. *Industry group rank.*

NOTES

1. William O'Neil, *How to Make Money in Stocks* (McGraw-Hill, NY, 1991).
2. *Ibid.*
3. C. Colburn Hardy, *The Investor's Guide to Technical Analysis* (McGraw-Hill, NY, 1978).
4. Justin Mamis and Robert Mamis, *When to Sell* (Simon & Schuster, NY, 1977).
5. *Ibid.*
6. *Ibid.*

7. Justin Mamis, *How to Buy* (Farrar, Straus, Giroux, NY, 1982). See also his books *When to Sell* (Simon & Schuster, NY, 1977) and *The Nature of Risk* (Addison Wesley, NY, 1991).

8. *Ibid.*

9. John Dennis Brown, *Panic Profits* (McGraw-Hill, NY, 1994).

10. Investor's Business Daily, *Guide to High-Performance Investing* (O'Neil Data Systems Inc., Los Angeles, 1993).

11. *Ibid.*

12. O'Neil, *How to Make Money in Stocks.*

13. *Ibid.*

14. Richard Russell, in *A Treasury of Wall Street Wisdom*, ed. Harry Schultz and Samson Coslow (Investor's Press Inc., Palisades Park, NJ, 1966).

15. O'Neil, *How to Make Money in Stocks.*

16. Charles Kirkpatrick II, interview, *Technical Analysis of Stocks and Commodities*, April 1995.

17. Richard Russell, in *A Treasury of Wall Street Wisdom*, ed. Schultz and Coslow.

18. Robert Colby and Thomas Meyers, *The Encyclopedia of Technical Market Indicators* (Dow Jones Irwin, Homewood, IL, 1988).

19. O'Neil, *How to Make Money in Stocks.*

20. *Ibid.*

21. James Collins, personal communication to *Investor's Business Daily.*

22. Richard Russell, in *A Treasury of Wall Street Wisdom*, ed. Schultz and Coslow.

23. Investor's Business Daily, *Guide to High-Performance Investing.*

24. *Ibid.*

25. *Ibid.* See also O'Neil, *How to Make Money in Stocks.*

26. O'Neil, *How to Make Money in Stocks.*

27. *Ibid.*

28. *Ibid.*

29. Investor's Business Daily, *Guide to High-Performance Investing.*

30. Phillip Fisher, *Common Stocks and Uncommon Profits* (PSR Publications, CA, 1984).

THE MONEY GAME[1]

Money is the patron and the object of the financial markets. The sole purpose of allocating capital to the financial markets is to make money. It has been said that in the battle for stock market profits, 90 percent of each battle is information.[2] Every investor in stocks, whether buyer or seller, arrives at a decision with what he or she *believes* is information. Not all information is factual, and opinions, estimates, analyses, and projections have all had their valid place in the hierarchy of investment sources. If all information were reliable and objective, the whole process of researching, analyzing, and developing investment systems would become unnecessary.[3] It is precisely this subjectivity of the investment process, the constant flux of human behavior and response, that has allowed a market to exist for trading stocks. And it is the volatility resulting from the market's subjectivity and consequent inefficiency that has provided investors with both its opportunities and its risks.

No one can win if everybody receives all the necessary information, understands it correctly and completely, and acts on it in a timely fashion.[4] Indeed, given the same information, no two investors will act on that information in the same way because people *are* different: Human responses have appeared to be as varied as humanity itself. Transactions in the market take place only because there is a difference of opinion, when both buyers and sellers back their own opinions, strongly if they feel confident, moderately if there are still a few doubts. The fallibility of the market is therefore expressed in the very action and nature of every trade. The result of these opposing views may be stationary prices, or a market fluctuating nervously within a narrow range, or a definite price movement in either direction, greater or smaller in proportion to the more or less emphatic preponderance of the buying or selling.

To participate in the investment process, the amount of money set aside for investing must be readily available, and the likelihood of needing it for other purposes must be very remote. An investment program is not a savings account: An advocated guideline has been that a working person should have available, as an emergency cash reserve in a savings account, between 3 to 6 months of living expenses before any investment proposal is even considered.[5] Guidelines for setting aside a portion of one's income regularly for a retirement fund have also been described.[6]

RISK-RELATED RETURNS

A foundational step in the investment process should be to set up the goals of a portfolio, no matter how small, and the rules to be followed for its investment. It is the investment goals that must shape the portfolio rather than have the portfolio control the investment philosophy.[7] It must also be realized at the outset that the financial markets are inherently unstable. Since few investment instruments can be relied upon to behave predictably, it becomes necessary to understand the level of uncertainty about the return expected from an investment, along with the frequency and amount by which a certain investment is likely to deviate from its targeted return.[8] It is the uncertainty regarding a proposed outcome, not the possibility of loss, that establishes the nature of risk in the financial world.[9] Investment performance is influenced by the risk taken: Assuming high risk in rising markets should generate excess returns, while doing so in falling markets magnifies the losses. Hence sound investment technique involves taking advantage of correctly identified bull market trends to increase the volatility of one's holdings, and reducing exposure to such variability at all other times.

An acknowledged goal of investment practice has been to direct the flow of money to investments that offer the highest

return relative to risk, and a preliminary step in the investment process is to assess the investment climate. This goal
requires, first of all, a determination of the return on an
investment with virtually no risk that would set the standard,
and then a means of comparing the risk-related returns of
other investment instruments with this standard and with one
another. U.S. Treasury bills, guaranteed as they are by the
U.S. government, have become the recognized standard of the
truly riskless investment. The accepted measure today of a
riskless return is the discounted rate (bid) on 90-day T-bills,
and this return sets the overall investment climate for assess-
ing the risk-related return expected on any investment. Since
T-bills have the lowest risk, they offer the lowest return, and
this return is the guaranteed minimum on investment that can
be obtained at any given time. Every other investment must
offer a higher return, since it carries a higher risk than T-bills.
And money should flow to the investment that offers the highest return relative to overall risk.

The competitive nature of the various investment instruments requires that a relative valuation system be available for
comparing risk-related returns between them. For financial
assets, this has traditionally been the measurement of *yield*,
which is the ratio of the return on the investment relative to
price—that is, yield = return on investment/price of investment.[10] For debt instruments (bonds), yield = interest
earned/price of bond. For shareholders who are equity owners
of a company, stock yield = corporate earnings/price of stock.
Some have placed more emphasis on dividends instead of
earnings, using a dividend yield (corporate dividends/price of
stock) instead of an earnings yield for stock valuation. Since
most stocks generally move together, it has become conve-
nient to use the broader stock market as a proxy for individual
stocks to compare stock values relative to interest rates.

ASSET ALLOCATION

Competitive valuation is a first step to understanding asset
allocation. Common areas that could be considered for invest-

ment include financial assets (stocks, bonds, money market instruments), real assets (real estate, precious metals), and tax-sheltered assets (municipal bonds). The distribution of funds among assets depends on the prevailing interest rate and inflation environment, and the current tax laws.[11] Real estate and precious metals have protected best against inflation; tax-sheltered assets offer tax savings advantages.

Among financial assets, stocks have generally allowed higher returns than bonds because of their higher investment risk. Between the years 1872 and 1992, for example, the annual return on U.S. common stocks averaged + 8.8 percent and those on 20-year government bonds averaged + 4.6 percent, with considerable variation between one decade and the next.[12] Over the same 120 years, the average annual total return on the riskless 90-day T-bills was only 3.7 percent. Hence the perils of being out of the stock and bond markets and staying only in T-bills or money market investments can be substantial in terms of opportunities lost. Between 1940 and 1948, and from 1973 to 1980, the real returns on T-bills, when corrected for inflation, were actually negative.[13] The risk-free investment in T-bills that traditionally formed the bedrock of investment returns was thus relegated by inflation into the realm of returns generally associated with speculative uncertainties!

Asset allocation deserves more thought than just the selection of individual stocks or bonds. About 94 percent of the total return of a professionally managed portfolio has been shown to result from the choice of asset classes and the percentage of funds allocated to various asset classes, and not from the choice of the individual securities.[14] A practice of asset allocation encourages long-term investing, often taking advantage of several business cycles. The historical trend of higher returns on stock investments dictates that the common-stock position in a portfolio should be as large as the tolerance for risk would permit. Investment in different asset classes offers protection against market risk; nonmarket risk is safeguarded by holding different stocks from different industries. The larger a portfolio, the more its value will move with the market.

The process of asset allocation does require, of course, that there be sufficient assets to justify their allocation. Before assets have accumulated sufficiently to even consider their assignments in different instruments, a single broadly diversified stock mutual fund, or a single stock index fund, could be the sole initial depository for investment funds.[15] Thereafter, assets can be expanded into bonds using a simple rule of thumb: The bond component of a total investment portfolio should roughly approximate the age of the investor.[16] Cash positions, given their low long-term returns, should be kept below a modest 10 percent. The stock/bond mix can be rebalanced at regular time intervals, or be managed to allow profits to run.

There has never been a universal formula for asset allocation, since each investor needs to organize his or her own portfolio to meet its policy of risk and return. However, the nature of investment goals, and the time frames necessary to meet them, could dictate the means to that end. Money is accumulated to be eventually spent. Typically, the early years of any long-term investment plan are accumulative and seek to build the capital needed later for distribution. In the accumulation phase, an expansive long-term outlook, coupled with the benefits of compound interest, should allow the greater focus to be on reward rather than risk.[17] Stock commitments in growth and value issues should predominate during these years with, depending on individual preferences, greater or lesser participation in small companies, specialized sectors, and the international scene. Bonds should be acquired through mutual funds that are limited to U.S. Treasuries, investment-grade corporate bonds, or, if warranted for tax shelter, highly rated municipal issues. Bond maturity should vary with the time horizon, but quality (high bond ratings) should not succumb to the temptations of higher income.[18] As the time for distribution draws near, risk must become a more dominant consideration than reward, and the portfolio should be gradually realigned to a reduced equity position not exceeding 35 percent to reflect this coming of age. Low-cost stock index funds, and bond funds with low fees and no loads, have been the mainstays for the income oriented.[19]

In the case of stocks, diversification reduces risk and improves return as long as stocks do not move in unison. This means purchasing stocks across industry groups. A completely undiversified portfolio of stocks would include only one stock, and the variability of such a portfolio has been estimated to be 40 percent annually.[20] At the other extreme, the ultimate in diversification would be to hold every stock in the market, and the variability of such an investment has been estimated to be 22 percent annually. Full diversification in the stock market therefore theoretically reduces portfolio risk in stocks by almost half. It has also been determined that a portfolio of 10 typical stocks provides 87 percent of the possible advantages of full diversification, and one of 20 such stocks provides 93 percent of the advantages.[21] Thus, for the individual investor, there is no great advantage or safety in holding a very large number of stocks. Indeed, unless the focus is concentrated on a small number of a few good stocks, perhaps fewer than 6 stocks, the scope for good performance is limited, and the performance of a portfolio of many stocks will be far more dependent on the movement of the overall market than on the investor's choice of stocks.[22]

Moreover, to gain the performance advantage today, investments should eventually take a global approach and diversify across asset classes and across the world, as well as across the securities in a particular asset class. Such a broad diversification has been shown to reduce dramatically the risk of a portfolio. Probability analysis has claimed that there is a 64 percent chance that stocks will outperform bonds in any 5-year period, with the likelihood rising to 76 percent over any 20-year period.[23] Hence, in any core portfolio, that portion allocated to higher-return objectives will normally find a higher proportion of total money devoted to the stock market.

THE CONDITIONS OF INVESTMENT IN STOCKS[24]

There is a potentially harmful mental attitude that often overcomes the novice investor, and that is a tendency to enter the stock market as if it were not played with real money. The market must be entered with the recognition that the money to be invested is at risk, and the first investment principle is that to survive in the market, the investor must *cut losses*. This rule, however obvious it may appear to be, is among the most important. It is a proper and prudent thing to do whether it be for the purpose of protecting one's profits or curtailing one's losses. There must be just as valid a reason for continuing to hold on to a stock as there was for purchasing it in the first place.[25] Losses must be restricted, because all it takes is one serious loss for the growth of an investment program to become compromised for many years.[26] In the battle for investment survival, the safety of one's principal must be secured first, before embarking on accumulating satisfactory returns.

Extensive testing has shown that the maximum amount that can be lost on a single stock investment without damaging long-term prospects is 2 percent of the total capital assigned to stocks.[27] The 2 percent rule ensures that even a few losing trades will not cripple the long-term prospects of the portfolio. The larger the investment account, the smaller this percentage should become. Some have advocated that a 7 percent price decline from the purchase price of a stock is the maximal loss that should be tolerated for each stock, and the position must be sold in such a situation;[28] others have based the fraction of capital to be put at risk on any single stock investment as a function of the overall performance of their investment system and the size of the investment account.[29]

An investment program must also insist on the *preservation of purchasing power*—that is, the ability to get income and principle repaid in units of the same purchasing power as originally invested.[30] Every purchase should be considered almost solely on the basis of what it will return in dividend income and price appreciation added together and treated as one. This can be ensured in two ways—first, by the care used in stock selection and, second, by the maintenance of a large cash reserve.[31]

It has been recommended that the size of commitments to stocks—namely, the ratio of funds employed to buy stocks compared with total portfolio capital—should be initially kept small,

at about 30 percent. Any program that involves complete investment of all capital at all times will most likely fail unless the
amount of it is very small. One should strive for a large profit
on a small cash commitment. No stocks of any kind should
under any circumstances be bought or retained under this policy unless, in the investor's judgment, the profit possibilities are
large and greatly outweigh the visible risks. This policy may
involve not only concentrating on very few stocks but also holding one's capital uninvested for long periods of time.
Sufficiently attractive opportunities to buy stocks arise only a
few times each year; in the interim, the market should be left
alone to shape itself for the next big movement.[32] Although
cash represents an investment with limited productivity, it also
possesses the desirable quality of risklessness.[33] The wisdom
that leads to its appropriate creation, plus the discipline to
resist the temptation to reconvert cash into an investment at
risk, has been a necessary attribute for profitable investing.[34]

Investment goals in the stock market should be set very high,
for only there lies safety. It is perhaps futile to try to get results
except by buying into anticipated large gains. Some would have
it that a position should not be entered unless the minimum
upside potential for a profit is three times greater than the
downside potential for a loss.[35] A program should be aimed at
obtaining a sufficient profit to offset the average losses sustained
in all investment resulting from the inevitable personal errors of
judgment, the effects of inflation and currency depreciation and
taxation, and the unexpected necessity of having sometimes to
close out an investment earlier than originally planned.[36]
However, it is rare even for market professionals to claim a legacy of *sustained* annual returns exceeding 25 percent. It has been
proposed that the investor should make it a rule that each time a
profitable trade has been closed, one-half of the profits should
be locked up in a safe fixed-income account.[37] No general keeps
his troops fighting all the time, nor does he go into battle without some part of his forces held back in reserve.[38]

It is also necessary to set, at the outset, an *absolute* rate of
expected return on any investment—that is, how much money
one can realistically earn or can afford to lose—rather than be

content with a *relative* rate of return wherein one's performance is compared with some benchmark index of the marketplace. Every effort must be made to stay aloof from the relative performance mindset. There can be neither joy nor consolation when a portfolio declines, even though the benchmark market averages may have swooned further. Relative performance is a self-defeating euphemism that can have the effect of validating questionable investment practices. It permits poor outcomes to become comforting rather than serve as a potential warning, and allows market risks to become masked. Though in the investment world it has been regarded as more praiseworthy to fail conventionally than to succeed unconventionally, no satisfaction should be drawn from the fact that others have performed worse.

TO DIVERSIFY (OR NOT TO)

No investment principle has been more widely commended than *diversification*. The horrors of what can happen to those who put all their eggs in one basket have been too constantly preached.[39] Nonetheless, the beginning investor who desires to build a portfolio *only in stocks* should strenuously adhere to a rule advocated by many worthy market professionals, namely, to concentrate in a few stocks only and follow those issues closely. A well-diversified portfolio of stocks should be one with a few good ideas that are all potentially profitable. There are, at any one moment, only a few stocks that can have a maximum potential, and even seasoned individual investors have often been unable to follow more than a handful of stocks at a time. Moreover, diversification often serves to limit portfolio growth because of the relatively small amounts of money accorded to each selection, with the profits of those well-selected issues being effectively offset by the relatively unsatisfactory results experienced by the others.[40] Likewise, no matter how good the profit possibilities, not more than 20 percent of funds should be delegated to any one situation. There is an axiom that a position so large as to cause insomnia should be reduced to the point of sound sleep.[41]

Overdiversification, by purchasing too many stocks, acts as a poor protection against lack of knowledge. Concentration in many ill-chosen issues could result in substantial losses, just as the same concentration in a few could have a very salutary effect. The prospects of an investment should be so good that placing a rather large proportion of one's total funds in a single outstanding situation should not seem excessively risky.[42] This means that diversification may be unnecessary.

One or two, or at most three or four, securities should be initially bought. A few relatively large blocks of shares are preferable to a great many small positions. A large number of small holdings tend to be purchased with less care, and are ordinarily allowed to run into a variety of small losses without full realization of the eventual total sum lost.[43] Failure to keep a discerning eye on the behavior of stocks in a portfolio is as unpardonable as using poor judgment in selecting them. It is mandatory to keep a finger on the pulse of each commitment. Concentration in a minimum number of stocks ensures that enough time will be given to the choice of each, so that every important detail about them will be known. And the stocks should be so well selected, their purchase so timed, and their profit possibilities so large, that it should never be necessary to risk in them a large proportion of available capital.[44]

WHEN YOU SELL ALSO COUNTS

The quest for profit can be fulfilled only if strategic purchases are compliemented by equally strategic sales.[45] There is no valid reason to continue to hold on to a stock and not sell it just because it was bought. A decision to retain a losing stock is no different from a decision to buy a loser.[46] Any arbitrary reason to validate the retention of a sharply falling stock can become a costly departure from reality, and the severity of the loss is generally in direct proportion to the length of time for which the issue of a falling stock remains unresolved.[47] There have been many who believe that opening a stock investment must be done on short-term principles, because short-term investing, once mastered, has much more of the elements of dependable business than do the uncertainties of the long pull.[48] No stock should be held indefinitely simply because no falling stock is a good stock.[49] It follows, therefore, that the entire investment process should be intermittent rather than continuous and should be pursued on a relatively intermediate-term basis. The length of time any stock should be held is dictated expressly by the behavior of the stock, and this calls for a habit of mandatory daily surveillance of stock action.

The individual investor must also beware that, if the intermediate-term method of investing is pursued, a company and its stock should never be considered to be identical. This is a subtle but critical mistake that must be strenuously guarded against.[50] A stock's price reflects the market's reactions and perceptions as expressed in buying and selling actions, and not the truths about the strengths of its underlying company. A stock and its issuing company often do not move together in harmony; there are times when a firm's business prospers but its shares decline in price, and vice versa. It is a dangerous practice to justify holding on to a falling stock instead of selling it by deflecting one's focus from the stock's declining price to the company's fundamental merits; there is only one reliable parameter that makes for consistent profits in the stock market, and that is a stock's price performance.[51] It is necessary to develop the mindset that in the intermediate-term method, one is trading the stock, not the company.

Trades should also never be closed unless a good reason is at hand. Recognizing and writing down the paramount reason to purchase a stock allows the singling out of the main reason to sell it. If the reason for which a stock was purchased has not worked out or has proved to be invalid, then the commitment must be dissolved. The intermediate-term method, therefore, requires the closing of a trade for a reason, and if later the situation changes, then one may reestablish the position. In any case, the risk of selling too early has never been as great, nor as uncomfortable to accept, as that of waiting too long.[52]

A MATTER OF DISCIPLINE

Successful investors, we are told, know that they have won the game even before they have started.[53] The great players play to win while all others try hard not to lose. By and large, many found early success in investment and then suffered major defeats in the markets, but went on to acquire legendary profits because of their perseverance and personal commitments. Besides having a driving desire to become successful, often overcoming significant obstacles, one must devote time to investment.

There has never been a method of trading successfully without taking many losses. Indeed, the definition of success in the stock market is to make more money than one loses. The investor must be as willing to admit a mistake in the event losses are sustained as desirous to claim personal credit in the realization of profits. This is not merely a question of prudence; it is also a mark of wisdom. And losses will occur, because the money game involves a predator-prey relationship in which the prey is also armed and on the hunt.[54]

The best of investment systems have been right in their selections only 30 percent to 50 percent of the time, and have needed to cut losses in the rest of the issues to remain successful. Although loss in the markets is absolute, the market, like life itself, has the advantage that opportunities keep coming along to make another choice, and then another.[55] The ability to sell out quickly and accept small early losses has been the cornerstone of many an investor's prosperity, and minor mishaps must be accepted speedily before they become painful. It is neither embarrassing nor self-deprecating to take a small loss; indeed, it has been, without question, evidence of far superior investment talent to take modest losses and leave the scene of impending disaster than to record less than mediocre performance by refusing to sell. Individual failure to achieve investment profits has nearly always reflected an unwillingness to sell in the hope that stocks already risen will continue to gain and provide the opportunity to make more money. Equally damaging is the failure to recognize an error by remaining wedded to a stock in which a loss has occurred in the hope that it will rise again. It is necessary to keep one's hopes out of the judgment process.

INVESTOR, KNOW THYSELF

When modern investment techniques have failed to achieve generalized success is the point at which analytical determinations of value and timing should be allowed a pause, and human factor involvement be assessed objectively. Part of the time devoted to study should include an analysis of one's own mistakes. Withdraw from the market for a while, and thus unburdened, sit down and analyze the decisions made over a period of time. Stop to ask what is known, whether what is known is enough, and how one is relating to it. Periodic self-examination is necessary to review whether new conditions have arisen which require a change of direction and pace, or whether one has lost sight of the essential problem. Whereas it is the strong points that determine one's potential in the marketplace, it is the weak points that determine the actual results.[56]

When individual investors enter the securities market with real money, it is essential that they know, and perhaps even write down on a real-time basis, the thoughts that went into the investment decision: why a stock was bought, why the market conditions and the market timing were considered to be a good buying point, what the expected return can be and how long it is expected to take, and what one was willing to risk.[57] This discipline helps cement the characteristics of a winning stock. There is usually only one predominant reason as to why a particular stock purchase can be expected to show a profit, and writing things down is the best way to identify this single factor.

Much can be learned by returning once more, after selling a losing stock, to the charts and notes made at the time of its purchase to review the information and ideas that prompted the trade, and try to understand why a loss occurred in that carefully planned situation.[58] Every loss represents a judgment error, be it in calling a market's trend or strength or its timing. Though it is true that every triumph sharpens the sting of later defeats, losing, in a curious way, can become winning if one has changed because of a loss and has taken away from it something one never had before. It has been said that those who cannot learn from their past are condemned to repeat it, and nowhere does this stand true more than in the marketplace. In the final analysis, it is simplicity, concentration, and a sense of what is vital that make up the qualities that distinguish a great investor. There has never been a holy grail to the money game.[59]

NOTES

1. Several outstanding books on the investment process have laid the foundation for this chapter. They reveal a broad spectrum of strategies and philosophies that together make up the variety of investment experiences, and it is their words and wisdom, accumulated over long periods of syntopical reading, that make up this text. The books are referenced below.

2. Gerald Loeb, *The Battle for Stock Market Profits* (Simon & Schuster, NY, 1971).

3. Peter Bernstein, *Capital Ideas* (Maxwell Macmillan Int'l, NY, 1991).

4. *Ibid.*

5. John Bogle, *Bogle on Mutual Funds* (Irwin Professional Publishing, NY, 1993).

6. Maria Crawford Scott, "How Much of Your Salary Do You Need to Save for Retirement?" *AAII Journal,* October 1994.

7. James Owen, *The Prudent Investor* (Probus Publishing, Chicago, 1990).

8. *Ibid.*

9. *Ibid.*

10. Lawrence Stein, *Value Investing* (John Wiley & Sons, NY, 1987).

11. *Ibid.*

12. Bogle, *Bogle on Mutual Funds.*

13. *Ibid.* Asset allocation and risk-reward analyses are lucidly discussed in this excellent investment manual. This paragraph, and the one following, have been put together from the ideas in Bogle's book.

14. Richard Brealey, *An Introduction to Risk and Return from Common Stock* (MIT Press, Cambridge, MA, 1982).

15. Bogle, *Bogle on Mutual Funds.*

16. *Ibid.*

17. *Ibid.*

18. *Ibid.*

19. *Ibid.*

20. Brealey, *Introduction to Risk and Return from Common Stock.*

21. *Ibid.*

22. *Ibid.*

23. Owen, *Prudent Investor.*

24. Several sources have been used to create this section. Primary are the two books by Gerald Loeb: *The Battle for Investment Survival* (Simon & Schuster, NY, 1956) and *The Battle for Stock Market Profits* (Simon & Schuster, NY, 1972). These classics contain the great truths and the great errors that have formed the basis of most investment systems. Many recent "best-sellers" in investment stem from the principles asserted here by this "wizard of Wall Street." The books, available as paperbacks, should be part of the foundation of any personal investment library.

25. Raymond Righetti, *Stock Market Strategy for Consistent Profits* (Nelson-Hall, Chicago, 1980).

26. "Adam Smith," *The Money Game* (Dell Publishing, Chicago, 1967).

27. Alexander Elder, *Trading for a Living* (John Wiley & Sons, NY, 1993).

28. O'Neil, *How to Make Money in Stocks.*

29. Elder, *Trading for a Living.*

30. Loeb, *Battle for Investment Survival.*

31. *Ibid.*

32. Jesse Livermore, *How to Trade in Stocks* (1940; reprinted by Indicator Research Group, Palisades Park, NJ, 1966).

33. Eric Emory, *When to Sell Stocks* (Dow Jones Irwin, Homewood, IL, 1973).

34. *Ibid.*

35. Victor Sperandeo, *Trader Vic II: Principles of Professional Speculation* (John Wiley & Sons, NY, 1995).

36. Loeb, *Battle for Investment Survival*.

37. Livermore, *How to Trade in Stocks*.

38. Bernard Baruch, *My Own Story* (Holt, Rinehart & Winston, NY, 1957).

39. Philip Fisher, *Common Stocks and Uncommon Profits* (PSR Publications, CA, 1984).

40. *Ibid*.

41. Conrad Leslie, *Guide for Successful Speculation* (Dartnell, Chicago, 1970).

42. Loeb, *Battle for Investment Survival*.

43. *Ibid*.

44. *Ibid*.

45. Righetti, *Stock Market Strategy for Consistent Profits*.

46. *Ibid*.

47. *Ibid*.

48. Loeb, *Battle for Investment Survival*.

49. Righetti, *Stock Market Strategy for Consistent Profits*.

50. Donald Cassidy, *It's Not What You Buy, It's When You Sell That Counts* (Probus Publishing, Chicago, 1991).

51. *Ibid*.

52. Leslie, *Guide for Successful Speculation*.

53. Jack Schwager, interview, *Technical Analysis of Stocks and Commodities*, 1994.

54. Thomas Herzfeld and Robert Drach, *High-Return, Low-Risk Investment* (New American Library, NY, 1983).

55. Justin Mamis, *The Nature of Risk* (Addison-Wesley, NY, 1991).

56. James Grant, *Minding Mr. Market* (Farrar, Straus, Giroux, NY, 1993).

57. Loeb, *Battle for Investment Survival*. See also George Soros, *The Alchemy of Finance* (Simon & Schuster, NY, 1987). O'Neil, *How to Make Money in Stocks*; and the interviews of William O'Neil and David Ryan in Jack Schwager, *Market Wizards* (Harper & Row, NY, 1989).

58. See interviews of David Ryan and William O'Neil in Schwager, *Market Wizards*.

59. "Adam Smith," *Money Game*.

PART TWO

ANALYSIS OF THE STOCK MARKET

ECONOMIC VITAL SIGNS

Because of its fundamental importance in the investment process, the entire first page of Section B in *Investor's Business Daily* is dedicated to *The Economy* to help focus on the big picture. Economic ideas are always and intimately a product of their own time and place.[1] They must change as the world changes if they are to retain their relevance. It is the changing economy that is predominantly reflected in the prices and yields of specific investments and in the behavior of general securities, and it is the changing economy that determines which investments are the most appropriate at specific times.[2]

The most important current events and ideas are summarized in fewer than five sentences each in the column *Economy Update*. A unique block on *Perspective* presents a scholarly debate on a controversial theme which is first clearly enunciated, and then argued with supportive evidence. These debates view economic thought and practice for what they really are: the steady elaboration and adaptation of economic ideas, both when they are right and when they are wrong, to the immediate practical world as it is known and understood.[3] The range of issues and concerns about which economists may ruminate is ultimately set by the constraints and possibilities imposed by the material and intellectual realities of the larger society.

The right side of this page is devoted to two main stories, one of which expands on the most significant current economic news release of that day, usually an economic or monetary indicator, that has already been graphically presented on the first page in the *Inside Today* block. The universe of the world economies is brought together in *World Economy in Brief*.

There is no limit to the time that can be spent on monitoring the economy. In the beginning, the individual investor could focus only on four main parameters and their trends: the business cycle (GDP), interest rates, inflation, and the foreign exchange rate.

THE BUSINESS CYCLE (GDP)[4]

Business cycles have been defined as a type of fluctuation found in the aggregate economic activity of those nations that organize their work mainly through private business enterprises.[5] For economic purposes, American business has been best represented by the dollar value of all the goods and services that are produced in the nation without distinction between the private and public (government) sectors. Such a dollar sum is also called the *gross domestic product* (GDP), so that business cycles, over the decades, have come to reflect the recurring rises and declines in the value of the GDP. Understanding the business cycle, therefore, has become an appreciation of the determinants and characteristics of the GDP, and the factors that cause it to vary from quarter to quarter.

It is not difficult to picture a business cycle, which, like any other cyclical activity, has a rising phase and a declining phase (Exhibit 4-1). The rising phase is called *expansion* and is measured by such indicators as rising production, employment, and business profits. It is followed by the declining phase, called *contraction,* which includes declining production, unemployment, and business losses. Whereas expansion represents the entire upward phase of the cycle, the initial rapid upturn starting from the lowest point of the cycle is commonly referred to as a *recovery.* When economic activity during a recovery exceeds the highest level attained during the entire upturn of the immediately preceding business cycle, then this additional growth is called an *expansion*. A compara-

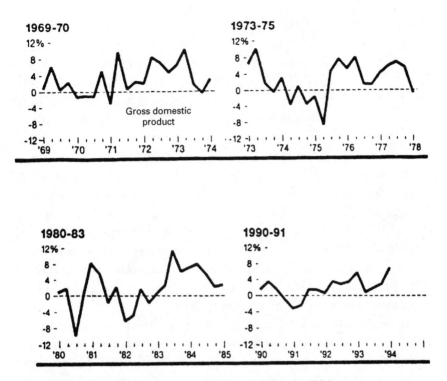

EXHIBIT 4-1. The U.S. Business Cycle: GDP 1969–1991.

ble sequence characterizes the downward phase of a business cycle. The immediate downturn constitutes a *recession,* and when activity during a recession falls below the lowest level of the previous downturn, this more depressed period becomes a contraction or *depression.* The highest point of an expansion before it turns downward to recession is the *peak,* and the lowest point of a recession before it turns upward to recovery forms its *trough.* A complete business cycle may be measured from trough to trough or peak to peak, but has been more commonly viewed from the trough of one contraction to the trough of the following contraction. It is therefore composed of a recession phase and an expansion phase. Expansions have been typical of the long-term U.S. economy, whereas true depressions have been rare.

It remains fundamental that changes in the GDP must represent growth or regression in the real economic activity of the nation, and not changes in prices.[6] As an example, suppose that an economy produces only oil, and that oil sold for

$10 per barrel in 1980 and $20 per barrel in 1990. Now suppose that the real output of oil had remained unchanged between these years at 1 billion barrels per year. GDP for 1980 would be $10 billion (1 billion barrels at $10 per barrel), but that for 1990 would appear to be doubled at $20 billion! Clearly this does not reflect true growth, but only the result of rising prices, since real oil production has remained unchanged. To remove inflation out of GDP in this example, it becomes necessary to use the same price, such as the 1980 prices, to compute the value of the output for both years. Any change in GDP would then be a real change, not one due to rising prices, and such an estimate is called the *real GDP*. If no adjustment is made for changes in prices, one would then be measuring what is called the *nominal GDP*. Real GDP is sometimes called GDP in constant dollars, and nominal GDP has been called GDP in current dollars.

An estimate of GDP can be put together by organizing the aggregate economy into four component sectors which include all the major areas of business endeavor. These categories are the household (consumer) sector, the business sector, the government sector, and the international sector. Each sector is made up of dozens of subcomponents. Each category is reported exclusively in terms of the dollar costs that reflect its intrinsic value in the marketplace. No consideration is given to the social or any nonmaterial worth of that category to the economy. It is the interdependencies among these categories that create the business cycle: Expenses in one sector become incomes to some of the other sectors. Households, for example, purchase manufactured consumer products from businesses and pay taxes to government, thus providing income to the business sector and to the government, respectively. Businesses, in their turn, provide income to households through wages or through dividend payments. Exports bring income into the country to benefit households, business, and government from goods and services that are domestically produced and are paid for by foreigners.

In its simplest form, GDP has been represented by the equation:

$$GDP = C + I + G + X$$

Where C = consumer spending
$\quad$ I = investment (business) spending
$\quad$ G = government spending
$\quad$ X = net exports (exports minus imports)

If total exports exceed total imports at any time, the difference is added to the GDP figure; if not, the difference is subtracted. The *retail sales* report is probably the most pertinent indicator in the consumer spending sector that the individual investor needs to understand, and the same applies for the *capital investment* and the *inventory* components of the business ("invesment") sector.

A turning point traditionally used to identify the peak of economic expansions and the trough of economic recessions is the change in direction of the real GDP. Although a variety of quarterly and monthly economic data are considered, a recession is usually defined as occurring when the quarterly real GDP (i.e., GDP in constant dollars) declines and remains negative for two quarters in a row. Since the first recorded expansion in December 1854, some 31 peaks and 32 troughs have been recognized up to 1992. Since 1945, an average expansion has lasted 45 months and an average recession about 11 months. Thus, business expansions in recent times have lasted about 4 times longer than recessions. A depression has occurred only twice in this century—in the 1930s and in 1981–82. It has been estimated that over the past 200 years, depressions have occurred at 30- or 60-year intervals.

FORECASTING A BUSINESS CYCLE

It would be undoubtedly advantageous to predict when the turns in a business cycle will occur, since most sustained and substantial swings in stock market prices have been closely associated with corresponding swings in the business cycle. However, forecasting these movements of aggregate economic activity has been a notoriously difficult task. Over the decades, research has uncovered series of statistical measurements that have behaved in a systematic way to conform reliably and regularly to turns in a business cycle. These series have become the basis for the construction of indexes which are classified according to the consistency with which they have led, coincided with, or lagged behind the turning points of a business cycle.

The composite index of *leading economic indicators* is the chief barometer used by the U.S. government to predict the turns in a business cycle. Although the leading indicators have consistently anticipated a recession or a recovery over the past 40 years, this has become known with certainty only by hindsight. The time lag from the peak of the leading indicators to the peak of a business cycle has been quite variable and unpredictable except as an average.

The index of leading indicators measures 10 components of the economy and is designed to forecast the direction of economic growth over the next 6 to 9 months. Some believe that it is more reliable for predicting activity only 1 to 3 months ahead. It is not concerned with predicting the amount of strength or weakness in the economy. Forecasting the upturns and downturns is the intended purpose of this index. Empirical track record has been important in the selection of a specific indicator.

The revised composite index of leading indicators issued by the Commerce Department in 1996 is constructed from the following components (Exhibit 4-2):

1. The yield curve
2. Delivery time as measured by vendor performance
3. Average weekly initial claims for state unemployment insurance
4. Contracts and orders for new plants and equipment, in 1982 dollars
5. Stock price index (S&P 500)
6. New factory orders for consumer goods and materials, in 1982 dollars

Leading Economic Indicators
By month (1987 = 100)

recessions

June: 102.9

Source: Conference Board

Investor's Business Daily

EXHIBIT 4-2.   The Composite Index of Leading Indicators.

7. Index of consumer expectations (University of Michigan)

8. Money supply (M 2) in 1982 dollars

9. New housing permits issued, index

10. Average workweek of workers in manufacturing

No individual indicator moves along a simple path, and the leading indicator index, which is smoother than most of its components and summarizes their movements, has become easier to follow. It has been advocated that turning points in an economy are generally signaled by three consecutive monthly changes of the leading index in the same direction, but this criterion has been shown to be frequently insufficient to forecast economic downturns. Moreover, it takes several months to be certain that 3 months of actual decline has indeed taken place. On average, the composite index has performed better at business cycle peaks than at troughs. The lead time for predicting business cycle peaks has been about 10 months while that for troughs has been only 2 months.

Whether or not the current economic performance is synchronized to the trend of future activity can be assessed by the index of the *coincident indicators* of economic performance. Coincident indicators measure current aggregate economic activity, and they rise and fall more or less together with the economy in a roughly coincident fashion. They indicate whether an economy is currently experiencing a slowdown and contraction, or a recovery and expansion. Coincident indicators have also been used to identify and date, after the fact, the peaks and troughs of a business cycle.

The index consists of four components:

1. Retail sales in constant dollars
2. Industrial production index
3. Number of employees on nonagricultural payrolls
4. Personal income less transfer payments in constant dollars

The index of *lagging indicators* affirms the future trend as predicted by the leading indicators, and confirms the current trend as expressed in the coincident indicators. Lagging indicators rise after an economy expands and fall after current economic activity has declined. The composite index of lagging indicators has the following components :

1. Average duration of unemployment
2. Ratio of business (manufacturing and trade) inventories to sales, in constant dollars
3. Labor cost per unit of output in manufacturing, monthly change
4. Average prime rate charged by banks
5. Commercial and industrial loans outstanding, in constant dollars
6. Ratio of consumer installment debt to personal income
7. Consumer price index for services, monthly change

The triad of composite indicators described above can indicate the current phase of a business cycle, but they are unable to signal when the business cycle is about to turn. This precision is provided by the *ratio of coincident to lagging indicators* (C/L ratio), which compares current with past economic activity to confirm, or refute, the future.[7] The indicator ratio has turned positive at business cycle troughs and negative at its peaks. Comparing the ratio with the leading indicators gives an idea as to whether the trend in future economic activity is peaking, or has already peaked.[8, 9]

NATURAL HISTORY OF THE COMPOSITE INDICATORS[9]

The primary bane of economic recessions is involuntary unemployment, and the Federal Reserve System (see later in this chapter) responds to this by increasing the money supply to stimulate the economy and the labor markets out of recession. The liberated money supply, available at the low interest rates and the low prices that had prevailed during the recession, renews consumer confidence. Consumers start to borrow money to make purchases, and rising consumer confidence leads the way out of an economic recession. The composite index of leading indicators begins to rise, along with the ratio of coincident to lagging indicators, to reach a peak.

Actual expansion of the economy presently follows, and a rising index of the coincident economic indicators indicates that a recovery is well under way. Shortly thereafter, the index of lagging indicators starts to climb. As the economic expansion reaches the midpoint of a business cycle, the demand for money and credit to finance the expansion also begins to accelerate. As the demand for goods and services increases, companies have to start paying higher prices for raw materials and deliveries. This rising cost of production is passed on to the consumer as higher shop prices (inflation). The rate of inflation rises as the economy approaches full employment and a high factory capacity utilization. As the expansion accelerates, overall confidence is typically high, the economy starts to outperform expectations, and inflation pressures begin to take a hold on a worrying Fed.

When money growth continues, the Fed begins to raise interest rates if only to retain the spread between real interest rates and the rate of inflation. Thus, higher rates of money growth in economic expansions result in higher interest rates. The Fed now moves into a posture of restricting monetary growth, thus driving interest rates even higher. However, because of time lags, it is virtually impossible for the Fed to quantify the restraint to precisely match the results desired to allow orderly economic behavior. Money growth targets are missed, and the economy moves into recession.

As the money supply peaks out and declines, the composite index of leading indicators and the C/L ratio peak out in their natural sequence and decline. A business cycle recession becomes likely when the composite index of leading indicators starts to decline over several periods. A recession is actually in place when the quarterly GDP has shown two consecutive downturns of negative growth. A decline in the composite index of coincident indicators inevitably follows, and the C/L ratio reaches a new low. The lagging index, which trails the economy and would still be rising, is the next to turn down. An early sign that the recession is easing would be an upturn in the composite index of leading indicators.

HOW TO USE *INVESTOR'S BUSINESS DAILY* TO MONITOR THE BUSINESS CYCLE[9]

The current phase of a business cycle is an aggregate picture of the economic activity that is in progress at the present time. It is put together by collecting and coalescing signals from various segments of the economy such as expenditures and incomes of households, businesses, and governments. These expenditures and incomes are interdependent: Expenditures in one segment become income to another segment.[10] In any approach to the business cycle, the first step should be to determine whether the economy is currently expanding or contracting. The second step should be to correctly recognize, during its expansionary phase, the onset, maturing, and waning of inflation.

The current phase of the business cycle, whether an expansion or a recession, can be determined in an accessible and condensed way by monitoring two sources: the quarterly GDP and the monthly composite indexes of the leading, coincident, and lagging economic indicators. The GDP is a retrospective indicator revealing what has happened to the business cycle during the previous quarters. The quarterly GDP report is presented in the *Inside Today* block on the first page of Section A of *Investor's Business Daily,* and is further evaluated in *The Economy* in Section B. It is reported as an annualized rate, using 1992 as the base period (real annual rate of change), and the graph tracks GDP over the last decade. A table in the same graph (Exhibit 4-3), or a separate table, lists the percentage changes in the GDP components during the current quarter and the immediately preceding one. However, comparing the current quarter only with the quarter immediately prior may lead to erroneous interpretations, because the volatile components of the GDP can create short-term irregularities. It is essential to understand how the revised GDP has progressed over the entire year, leading to its most recent report. For this reason, *Investor's Business Daily* also presents, from time to time, the long-term trend of the four main GDP components.

The composite index of the 10 leading indicators is presented graphically each month in the *Inside Today* block on the first page and in *The Economy* section. It is reported as an index number using 1987 as a base period (1987 = 100). Several years of data, and the percentage changes over the past 3 months, are shown on the graph to allow the recognition of trends. The graph is accompanied by a table which lists the net contribution of each component indicator. For example, when the indicator rose 0.5 percent in February 1993, 6 of its 11 components posted gains, 4 were negative, and 1 was unchanged. Consumer expectations, stock prices, and money supply reflect the psychological components of the index, while the remainder form its fundamental components. Since the index is released on the last business day of the month on the basis of the prior month's information, data on 9 of its 11 components are already

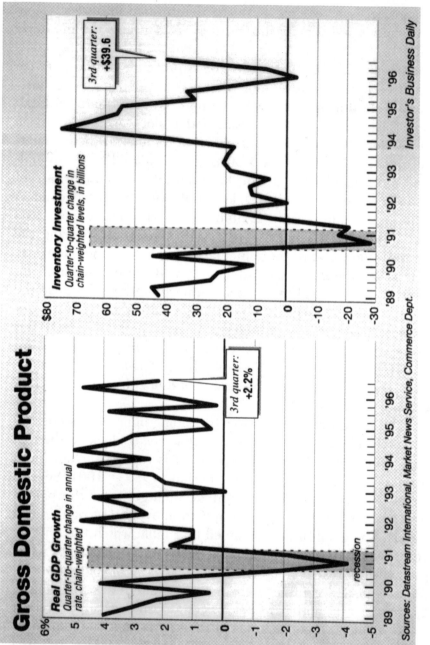

EXHIBIT 4-3. The GDP and Its Components.

Consumer Spending

Quarter-to-quarter change in annual
rate, chain-weighted

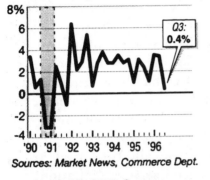

Sources: Market News, Commerce Dept.

Real 3Q GDP Summary

Chain-weighted	3Q advan.	2Q final
GDP	**+2.2%**	**+4.7%**
Current-$ GDP	+3.8	+6.5
Chain-wt. Price Index	+1.9	+2.2
Final Sales (Prod.)	+0.3	+4.1
Final Sales (Purch.)	+1.2	+4.7
Consumption	+0.4	+3.4
Nonres. fixed invest.	+14.7	+3.8
Inventories ($Bln)	+$39.6	+$7.1
Net exports ($Bln)	-$132.2	-$114.7
Gov't Purchases	-1.4	-1.4
Implicit Price Dfl.	**+1.6**	**+1.8**

EXHIBIT 4-3. (*CONTINUED*) The
GDP and Its Components.

known through previous releases during the month, and the
remaining 2 components can be estimated fairly accurately. This
allows the report to be forecast reasonably accurately, and financial markets therefore seldom react to its release unless it is sur-
prisingly different from market expectations.[11]

A report on the index of coincident indicators is presented in
The Economy section when released each month. The C/L ratio
is also presented from time to time in *The Economy* section,
especially when its value has reached a new high or a new low.

THE FEDERAL RESERVE SYSTEM

Money in the United States is created in the banking system. The ability of banks to actually create money, however, is determined by the Federal Reserve System, which was established by Congress in 1913 to be the nation's central bank and to stabilize the workings of the money and credit markets. By 1963, the Federal Reserve's objectives had been expanded "to help counteract inflationary and deflationary movements, and to share in creating conditions favorable to a sustained high level of employment, a stable dollar, growth of the country, and a rising level of consumption."[12] Ideally, this means trying to ensure that the prices of goods and services (inflation) rise no more than between 2.75 percent and 3.5 percent each year while the economy, as measured by GDP, grows between 2.25 percent and 2.75 percent, and unemployment remains just above 6 percent. The Federal Reserve regulates the amount of money and credit available for lending and the cost at which this credit can be attained.

The nation is divided into 12 districts, each with a Federal Reserve Bank. The banks in turn are coordinated by a 7-member Federal Reserve Board in Washington. The members of the Federal Reserve Board are also permanent members of a Federal Open Market Committee (FOMC). The Federal Reserve System regulates the nation's flow of money through the Federal Reserve Board and the FOMC, which together have commonly been referred to as the Fed.

THE MONEY SUPPLY

The amount of money available to the public through the banking system is called the money supply. It is measured under three categories, each of which builds on the items in the previous category to represent an increasing number of assets. The first of these components, labeled *M1*, includes only those assets such as currency, checking accounts, and traveler's checks which can be immediately used without restriction at any time to pay any amount to anyone. *M2* represents about 80 percent of the total money supply. It includes M1 plus liquid assets which are almost as good as money. Examples are savings accounts and shares of money market funds which can be easily withdrawn for the purchases of goods and services. It does not count deposits of $100,000 or more. Since the public can now use interest-bearing savings accounts as if they were demand deposits, and can shift cash between these demand deposits and other financial assets such as stock or bond mutual funds to seek the best return on investment, it has become difficult to maintain a distinction between these M's. *M3* includes both M1 and M2 and has no $100,000 limitation, and also counts additional assets such as repurchase agreements. M1 is the most liquid and can be converted to cash with minimal loss in value, and each successive component is less liquid.

THE CONTROL OF MONEY SUPPLY RESERVE REQUIREMENTS

Since 1980, banks belonging to the Federal Reserve System have been required to operate on what is called a *fractional reserve system,* whereby they are legally mandated to maintain, at all times, a certain specified fraction of all demand deposits as a cash reserve. This reserve can be either held on hand in the bank's own vaults as currency or coins or deposited with the Federal Reserve at district reserve banks. These required cash reserves are called *reserve requirements,* and their amount is set by the Federal Reserve. The reserves cannot be used by the depository institution for its usual business transactions. A bank can use for business transactions only the cash and check deposits it does not put aside for its required reserves.

The growth and control of the money supply by the Fed can now be understood against this background of the Fed's requirement for cash reserves (reserve requirements). Money supply grows when banks make loans. Here's how the system works.

Bank loans create new demand deposits or credit an existing demand deposit since, almost without exception, customers who get a bank loan initially deposit that money into a new or existing bank account on which they can subsequently write checks. And, as defined earlier, is not the bulk of money supply (M1 and M2) the money present in demand deposits? Whenever the amounts in demand deposits are increased, then, by definition, the money supply is increased. Thus, the first and essential step in creating money is taken by borrowers. If no one borrowed, no money would be created, regardless of the intentions of the bankers or the bureaucrats. The more the banks lend, the more demand deposits they create, and the greater becomes the money supply.

Thus, when a bank makes loans, it is not merely lending money; it is actually *creating* money as defined by M1 and M2. Ironically, it is not the deposits that allow banks to make loans; rather it is the bank lending that creates the deposits. Some loans *are* made on the strength of a bank's savings deposits, and to this extent it is savings that provide the fuel for the extension of credit. And since bank lending creates money supply, whoever can control bank lending (or bank credit) can control the supply of money.

One of the mechanisms whereby the Fed has controlled bank credit is by establishing the reserve ratios for the different categories of banks within limits set by Congress. Reserve requirements have the effect of controlling the amount of lending that banks can legally undertake. If the Federal Reserve wishes to limit the supply of money available to banks for lending, it raises reserve requirements so that more money must be kept on hand as reserves, and less is available for business and lending. The higher the level of reserve requirements, the more restricted becomes the ability of banks to lend money. For example, if a bank has to keep an arbitrary 20 percent of the money in reserves, it can lend out only 80 percent of what it has to consumers and business. If the reserve requirement were to drop arbitrarily to 10 percent, then the bank could lend out 90 percent of its money and the money supply would be higher. Because of its broad effects on the entire banking system, changing reserve requirements has been a strategy used by the Fed only on those rare occasions when it has determined the supply of money to be so seriously short, or so dangerously excessive, as to require remedy on a nationwide basis.

THE FED DISCOUNT RATE

Seasonal demands for money or short-term liquidity needs, among other things, often cause banks to usurp some of the money intended for reserves, which then fall below the legally required minimum. In these instances, banks have the option of borrowing the difference from the Federal Reserve itself to bring up their individual reserves to the legally required amount. The Federal Reserve charges interest for lending reserves. This interest, charged at the Fed's "discount" window, where a bank can borrow small amounts of money to cover a small deficiency in its reserves, is called the *discount rate*. The component of total reserves that are borrowed at the discount window by the banking system as a whole is called *borrowed reserves*. Banks cannot borrow large sums of money at the discount window to expand their individual business operations.

The Federal Reserve can make it either more difficult or more attractive for banks to borrow money at the discount window by either raising or lowering the discount rate. Changes in the discount rate tend to influence the entire structure of short-term interest rates. High discount rates tend to discourage banks from dipping into their cash reserves, thus making less money available for loans; furthermore, the banks' high cost of borrowing is passed on to the consumer or investor as higher general interest rates. Thus, the Federal Reserve can try to manipulate the discount interest rate as another means of controlling bank loans and, hence, the money supply.

THE FED'S OPEN-MARKET OPERATIONS

The third, and most frequently used, means employed by the Federal Reserve to control bank credit, and hence the money supply, is through its *open-market operations*. This technique has allowed the Fed to change the supply of bank reserves and eventually the money supply in a different way—namely, by buying and selling U.S. Treasury securities in the open market.

When the Fed decides to tighten the money supply, it *sells* from its store of U.S. Treasury securities to private dealers who make a market in such issues. The dealers pay for these securities with checks drawn on their accounts in their respective financial institutions (banks). However, the Federal Reserve collects from these institutions by reducing their respective reserve accounts at their regional Federal Reserve banks by the amount of the purchase. In effect, the Fed substitutes the cash that these banks are holding at the Fed with the U.S. Treasury securities. This step removes cash from these banks and reduces their general lending ability, thus leading to a tightening of the money supply. On the other hand, if the Fed decides on a more expansionary monetary policy, it *purchases* government securities from the dealers, who are then paid by crediting the sale to the reserve accounts of their banks.

BANK RESERVES: THE EFFECTS OF FED MONETARY POLICY

Prudent banks do not risk falling short in the reserve account and therefore hold reserves above and beyond the required amount. These additional balances in the form of cash or deposits at the Federal Reserve which are greater than the minimum required by law are called *excess reserves*. The sum of required reserves plus excess reserves constitute the *total reserves* present in the banking system. If the banking system has borrowed money from the Fed's discount window to make up its required reserves account, then the amount that has been borrowed is called the *borrowed reserves*. When the total amount of discount window borrowing is subtracted from total reserves, the balance is called *nonborrowed reserves*. The banking week ends on Wednesday, and the aggregate reserve position for the past 2 weeks is then reported in *Investor's Business Daily* (Exhibit 4-4). It is the nonborrowed component on the supply side that the Fed can influence through its open-market operations.[13]

THE FED FUNDS RATE

In the banking world today, deposit flows are constantly changing, resulting in routine excesses or shortages occurring each day in a bank's reserves. Banks blessed with excess reserves on a certain day lend them overnight to those experiencing a deficit. The interest rate charged for these overnight loans between banks is called the *federal funds rate*. Banks prefer to avoid the discount window, since repeated borrow-

Federal Reserve Data

Federal Reserve Weekly Data (in millions of dollars)				BANK RESERVES:			
MONEY SUPPLY:				Excess Reserves	$1,199	$1,195	$4
				Borrowed from			
	Latest	Previous	Change	Federal Reserve	$45	$95	-$50
M1	$1,140,800	$1,139,200	$1,600	Net Free or Borrowed			
Growth Percentage				(-) Reserves	$1,154	$1,100	$54
	13	26	52	**FACTORS AFFECTING BANK RESERVES:**			
	weeks	weeks	weeks	Float Credit	$1,408	$1,071	$337
M1	7.2%	8.7%	9.9%	Currency in			
M2	$3,571,200	$3,565,200	$6,000	Circulation	$365,796	$364,993	$803
M3	$4,199,700	$4,197,100	$2,600	Treasury Deposits	$5,222	$4,435	$787
				U.S. Government			
CREDIT DEMANDS:				Securities	$333,846	$333,050	$796
New York	Latest	Previous	Change	Federal Agency			
Bank Loans	$37,753	$37,400	$353	Obligations	$4,237	$4,314	-$77
Commercial Paper:				Loans to Depository			
Financial	$416,189	$418,161	-$1,972	Institutions	$24	$44	-$20
Non-Financial	$154,469	$151,728	$2,741	Includes: Seasonal			
Total	$570,658	$569,889	$769	Borrowings	$15	$15	$0
				Extended Credit	$0	$0	$0

EXHIBIT 4-4.   The Weekly Federal Reserve Data.

ings from the Fed might indicate reserve problems and could provoke an audit by the Federal Reserve. Banks, therefore, preferentially borrow in the overnight "fed funds" market.

When the banking system *as a whole* becomes deficient in its reserve requirements, the only option available to banks is to borrow from the Fed at the discount window. Thus, when the Fed tightens reserve availability to this extent through its open-market sales of U.S. government securities, it forces banks that are hard-pressed for funds to borrow temporarily at the discount window. A rising share of borrowed reserves, in relation to total reserves, represents a tightening in reserve pressures for the banking system as a whole. The magnitude of the changes in discount window borrowings (borrowed reserves) is therefore an early indicator of the direction and intent of Fed policy. And bank free reserves (i.e., excess reserves minus borrowings) have served as an even better indicator of Fed policy intentions than borrowings alone.

Since the Fed places limitations on access to the discount window, banks compete for and bid up rates on Fed funds. Therefore, for any given level of the discount rate, a rising total of borrowed reserves will be associated with a rising Fed funds rate. Conversely, a decline in borrowed reserves during periods when the Fed is easing reserve pressures will be associated with a falling Fed funds rate.

A significant rise in discount window borrowings will almost instantly be reflected in an upward move in the Fed funds rate. This mechanism allows the Fed to effectively set an upper and lower limit on the Fed funds rate. And since the discount rate is determined per se by the Federal Reserve, it can, by the above mechanism, effectively set the Fed funds rate and consequently influence all domestic short-term interest rates. The discount rate and the Fed funds rate are, therefore, closely linked in this manner (Exhibit 4-5).

HOW TO USE *INVESTOR'S BUSINESS DAILY* TO MONITOR THE FEDERAL RESERVE

Effective monitoring of the Fed is an art that requires developing a sense of the intent of monetary policy by monitoring the

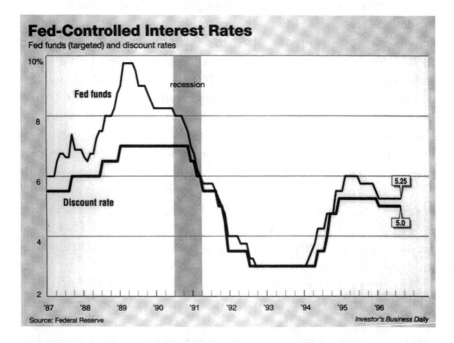

EXHIBIT 4-5. The Fed Funds Rate and the Fed Discount Rate.

same economic indicators that are tracked by the Fed to for-
mulate a policy decision, and then following other indicators
that provide an early signal of the Fed's response.[14] Fed policy
shifts should be viewed as a reaction to, rather than a cause
of, undesired economic or monetary fluctuations: For the
most part, the market leads the Fed rather than vice versa.[15]
The monetary process is a continuous one based on continuous readings of incoming economic and monetary data; it is
partly reactive to, and partly anticipatory of, trends in economic growth and price stability. The Fed evaluates and then
responds, and the secret of profitable monitoring of the Fed is
to follow, for a period of at least the preceding 6 months, the
key indicators that the Fed tracks, and then try to anticipate
the next Fed move. It is this next Fed policy change, usually
expressed through its open-market operations, that will be discounted in the bond and stock markets.

The *intentions* underlying the Fed's open-market operations are reflected in the movement of the *Fed funds interest
rates,* which indicate whether the immediate goal of monetary
policy is to stimulate or restrain the economy. The Fed funds
rate is the centerpiece of the money market and the entire
bond market because it links Fed policy shifts to bond yields
and stock prices and ultimately to fluctuations in economic
activity.[16] Monitoring the Fed funds rate has also offered a
reliable and early way to know what has transpired at the 6-
weekly meetings of the Federal Reserve Board, and what monetary policy may be in the offing.

The Fed funds rate (high, low, and closing values) is
reported at the bottom of the page facing that on *Credit
Markets* in a table called *Money Rates* (Exhibit 4-6). The
trend of the movement of the Fed funds rate is shown in a
chart entitled *Select Interest Rates* at the upper-right section
of the same page (Exhibit 4-7). Here, the 3-year trends of
the three commonly followed domestic short-term money
rates—namely, the Fed funds rate, the discount rate, and
the rate on 3-month Treasury bills—are shown together to
allow their comparison. Their combined chart curves present a clear picture of the current stage of the short-term
interest rate cycle.

Money Rates

Prime Rate...8.25	Commercial Paper (range):	Eurodollar Rates:
Base interest rate charged by major U.S. commercial banks on loans to corporations.	Dealers:	(Secondary Market)
	30-180 days 5.35-5.40	Overnight.............................5.125-5.1875
Discount Rate 5.00	Corporate Issuers:	1 month................................5.25-5.3125
Rate charged by Federal Reserve System on loans to depository institutions.	30-270 days............................5.25-5.24	3 months..............................5.375-5.4375
	Discount rate for unsecured notes of top-	6 months................................5.4375-5.50
Federal Funds Rate:	credit corporations sold directly or through	1 Year..................................5.5625-5.625
High 5.1875 Low 5.125 Close 5.125	dealers.	Rates paid on dollar deposits outside the U.S.
Rates on overnight loans among financial institutions.	Certificates of Deposit (Primary):	London Interbank Offered Rates:
	($100,000 minimum)	3 months 5.50
Bankers Acceptances:	30 days 4.48	6 months..5.54688
30 days...5.24	90 days 4.84	1 year 5.6875
60 days...5.30	180 days 5.02	The average of rates paid on dollar deposits.
90 days...5.28	Rates paid on new certificates of major	Treasury Bill Auction Results:
120 days...5.28	commercial banks, usually in blocks of $1	3 months (as of Nov. 4)...................5.04
150 days...5.29	million or more.	6 months (as of Nov. 4)...................5.08
180 days...5.29	Broker Call Loans 7.00	52-week (as of Nov. 7)....................5.20
Discount rate on business credits backed and sold by banks to finance trade.	Rate charged on short-term loans to broker- age dealers backed by securities.	Average discount rate for Treasury bills in minimum units of $10,000.
		Source: Dow Jones Telerate

EXHIBIT 4-6. Money Rates.

This chart also permits the difference between the Fed funds rate and discount rate, or the Fed funds rate–discount rate spread, to be examined (Exhibit 4-7). Both these rates represent the costs of borrowing to the banks. Changes in the difference between the rates often show a strong correlation to long-term movements in the stock market. Usually, the Fed funds rate slightly exceeds the discount rate. When Fed funds do not exceed the discount rate by more than half a point, or when the Fed funds falls below the discount rate, the climate is favorable for stock prices to rise higher.[17] The discount rate can be monitored in the same charts as the Fed funds rate. Changes in the discount rate over the last decade are shown every day in a small box on the *Market Charts* page (see Exhibit 1-5, Chapter 1).

The investor should note the current Fed funds rate. If the Fed funds rate drifts below the current rate over the next several weeks, then the Fed may be trying to stimulate the economy by adding money to the banking system to provide more funds for loans to consumers and businesses. Easing monetary policy would be associated with sharp falls in the funds rate. On the other hand, upward movements in the Fed funds rate raise the cost of borrowing, indicating a tightening in Federal

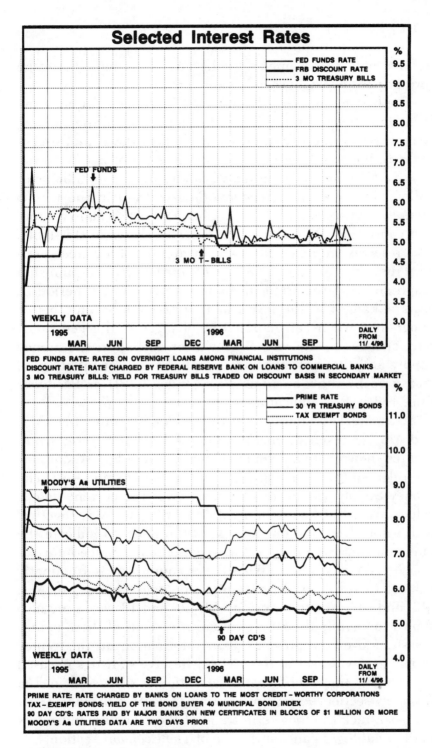

Selected Interest Rates

%
9.5
9.0
8.5
8.0
7.5
7.0
6.5
6.0
5.5
5.0
4.5
4.0
3.5
3.0

FED FUNDS RATE
FRB DISCOUNT RATE
3 MO TREASURY BILLS

FED FUNDS

3 MO T–BILLS

WEEKLY DATA

1995   MAR JUN SEP DEC   1996 MAR JUN SEP   DAILY FROM 11/ 4/96

FED FUNDS RATE: RATES ON OVERNIGHT LOANS AMONG FINANCIAL INSTITUTIONS
DISCOUNT RATE: RATE CHARGED BY FEDERAL RESERVE BANK ON LOANS TO COMMERCIAL BANKS
3 MO TREASURY BILLS: YIELD FOR TREASURY BILLS TRADED ON DISCOUNT BASIS IN SECONDARY MARKET

%
11.0
10.0
9.0
8.0
7.0
6.0
5.0
4.0

PRIME RATE
30 YR TREASURY BONDS
TAX EXEMPT BONDS

MOODY'S Aa UTILITIES

90 DAY CD'S

WEEKLY DATA

1995   MAR JUN SEP DEC   1996 MAR JUN SEP   DAILY FROM 11/ 4/96

PRIME RATE: RATE CHARGED BY BANKS ON LOANS TO THE MOST CREDIT – WORTHY CORPORATIONS
TAX – EXEMPT BONDS: YIELD OF THE BOND BUYER 40 MUNICIPAL BOND INDEX
90 DAY CD'S: RATES PAID BY MAJOR BANKS ON NEW CERTIFICATES IN BLOCKS OF $1 MILLION OR MORE
MOODY'S Aa UTILITIES DATA ARE TWO DAYS PRIOR

EXHIBIT 4-7.   Select Interest Rates.

Reserve policy. Movements of the Fed funds rate should be corroborated by changes in bank free reserves.

The best monitor for the *effects* of Fed policy has been the level, and changes in the level, of free reserves in the banking system. Bank reserves statistics are broken down into excess reserves, borrowed reserves, and net free (+) or net borrowed (−) reserves, and are reported weekly, expressed in millions of dollars, in the table of *Federal Reserve Data* in the *Credit Markets* section (Exhibit 4-4). Changes in the main factors that can influence bank reserves are also shown in this table. Free reserves are reported as a daily average of a 2-week period. From time to time, *Investor's Business Daily* will publish a graph showing the trend in bank reserves over a period of years. Changes in the levels of free reserves become better understood when corroborated by changes in the Fed funds rate, changes in the rate of growth or decline in the money supply and the monetary base, and changes in inflation as measured by the Consumer Price Index (CPI) or Producer Price Index (PPI) indicators.

Every week, a summary of the money measures M1, M2, and M3 is presented in the table of *Federal Reserve Data*. Figures shown here are compiled on the preceding Wednesday and released the following day, on Thursday (Exhibit 4-4). The Money Supply section in this chart gives the current (*latest*) value, in millions of dollars, of M1, M2, and M3, together with values from the previous week (*previous*) to indicate the direction and magnitude of the weekly change. Since information on M1 is gathered from fewer sources, it is frequently subject to substantial revision. Percentage changes of M1, M2, and M3 over the previous 52, 26, and 13 weeks are also shown to identify the long-term growth trends of these money measures over the previous year. Information on the money supply or any aspect of the Federal Reserve statistics released on that day that merit special attention is discussed in *The Economy* section. From time to time, *Investor's Business Daily* will also track the long-term trend of the monetary indicators in the *Vital Signs* panel at the top of *The Economy* section.

INFLATION

The price of particular goods is the amount of money for which one unit can be purchased or exchanged. The rate at which the general level of prices of goods and services is changing in an economy is called the rate of *inflation*. Inflation simply means a rising level of prices for consumer goods, services, commodities, and raw materials—rising because domestic residents are demanding more than the domestic economy can produce. In this definition, it is assumed that, over the time period wherein the prices of goods and services have changed, their quality has remained unchanged.

Prices of different goods may change at different rates, and this situation has been averaged by calculating the change in the amount of money required to buy a representative basket of goods. Different indexes of measuring inflation have result-ed from putting different goods and services into a basket, because no market basket can be the same to different people at any given time.

Although the price of a chosen basket could be quoted in money terms, it has been usual to express it as an index num-ber whereby the cost of the basket in some particular year, referred to as the base year, is arbitrarily set to equal 100. The index in the sense used here is a weighted average, and the weights reflect the importance of the included items to an average family; that is, they reflect the percentage of total household expenditure spent on each of the various categories of goods and services which an average household buys.

It is necessary that the measurement of the rate of infla-tion be expressed as a change in the price index per unit of time quoted—that is, as so many percentage points per year—rather than as an absolute rate of change. An absolute rate of change would be meaningless, since the initial value of 100 assigned to the index is a purely arbitrary one. Thus, the rate of inflation can be calculated for any given year by subtracting last year's (1996) price index from this year's (1997) index, dividing the difference by last year's (1996) index, and then multiplying the result by 100 to express it as a percentage. Furthermore, in an open economy that engages in international trade, some of the goods produced are exported in exchange for imports of goods to be used by domestic residents, and the relative prices of imports and exports are liable to change. Inflation has also been measured not by how much a particular basket of goods now costs, but by how much less a dollar bill can now buy. Charts showing the purchasing power of $1 compared with a chosen base year have been used by politicians with telling effect.

THE MEASURES OF INFLATION[18]

Every production process begins with the acquisition of raw materials or commodities which are processed by labor to make the finished product that is sold by manufacturers at the wholesale level, and bought by consumers at the retail level. Commodities are the simplest building blocks of all production: the fuels, metals, and grains that are the sources of all things made. Commodity prices are therefore the rawest and earliest measures of inflation.[19] A rise in commodity prices gets transmitted across the entire manufacturing process to the consumer, and commodity prices have often provided a preview, months ahead, of forthcoming changes in retail prices.

There are two types of commodity indexes. The first, called *spot price indexes,* reflect cash prices that need to be paid to purchase various commodities on the spot on that day. The other type, called *futures indexes,* tracks commodities that are bought on a sort of layaway plan whereby a contract is secured to buy a commodity at some future date at today's price. Both types of indexes move in tandem, but financial markets focus more on the futures indexes because they are more forward-looking. The most prominent of the futures indexes is the *CRB Futures Index* (Exhibit 4-8). Commodity prices also have a closer relationship to trends in long-term bond yields than does any other comparable factor.

Since commodities are traded globally, their prices represent international demand pressures. Moreover, currency

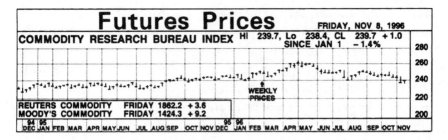

EXHIBIT 4-8.   The CRB Futures Index.

shifts can distort the significance of commodity price changes substantially for different nations. In mid-1994, for example, the *Journal of Commerce*'s basket of 18 industrial commodities was up 10.5 percent for U.S. purchasers. This dollar-denominated rise was more related to the weakness in the dollar than to escalating global inflationary pressures. The same basket had risen only 1.1 percent for German buyers, and had actually fallen 4.4 percent for Japanese purchasers because of a strong yen. Volatile commodity prices can, therefore, give very false signals of impending inflation, and their trend must be corroborated by other measures of domestic inflation.

Commodity prices should, for example, be related to *factory capacity utilization*. A rise in commodity prices during an economic expansion is not worrisome if there are no capacity shortages. It simply reflects the pickup in industrial activity that goes with expansion, and such a rise is unlikely to generate faster inflation at the manufacturing level. This is particularly true today, when raw materials account for less than a third of production costs. In fact, there has been almost no correlation between movements in the CPI and the CRB Index over the last 14 years.

On the other hand, employment costs can contribute to as much as two-thirds of total production costs, and there has been a close association between unit labor costs and movements in the CPI. It appears that with the changing economy today, labor costs have become a more important predictor of inflation than commodity prices. The *labor market*, examined in terms of unit labor costs, can provide better key signs of impending inflationary pressures in the form of rising payrolls, dropping jobless rates, replacement of part-time workers by full-time jobs, and high factory workweek figures. Trends in commodities should, therefore, also be correlated with growth in wages, rapid *money growth*, and some key indicators of inflation expectations such as the *yield curve, exchange rates*, and even *gold prices*. A rise in *housing prices* to record levels, for example, is additional evidence that inflation is at hand.

Producer prices (*Producer Price Index*) measure the cost of goods during production at the semifinished and finished manufacturing levels plus the rising costs of labor and materials to the business sector. They pick up changes in prices earlier than consumer price indexes, which concentrate mainly on retail goods. Prices at the retail consumer level (*Consumer Price Index*), or shop prices, are consumption-centered, and say nothing about wages or other income or investment returns. They do reflect government taxation and pricing policies, and are sensitive to tax changes and changes in mortgage interest rates. For example, alcoholic drink and tobacco prices may reflect as much the level of taxation as the costs of manufacture, and housing costs have always reflected the prevalent levels of interest (mortgage) rates. To get behind this aspect of retail prices requires working with an index of wholesale prices, or even going a stage further back to the price of raw materials and labor.

The most comprehensive measure of inflation is the *GDP price deflator*, because GDP is the most comprehensive measure of everything that is produced in the nation, well beyond the confines of goods and services bought by households. However, this indicator is released only quarterly, is frequently revised, and reflects the past rather than current trends. Most present indexes of inflation are biased upward because of unsatisfactory methods for adjustments in quality improvements in the goods and services produced. This technical problem of adequate adjustment for changes in quality has been difficult to surmount, since quality enhancements over time cannot be measured precisely. Many apparent price rises have been, in reality, higher prices for merchandise of better quality rather than higher prices for the same goods and services.

In interpreting the variety of measures of inflation, different indicators can paint a somewhat different picture. This occurs because some measures such as the CPI reflect *past* inflation, whereas others such as scrap metal prices, commodity prices, the purchasing managers' price indexes, and the spread between long- and short-term interest rates are forward-looking. The latter reflect expectations of future price levels led by those commodities that support the sectors of the economy which, if growing strongly, can lead to inflation: automobiles, housing, exports, and capital spending. The earliest signals of inflation arise from surveys of industry insiders, such as the National Association of Purchasing Managers, and from regional polls from the Federal Reserve Banks and private business groups.

LIMITATIONS OF INFLATION MEASURES

Dramatic and far-reaching structural changes in the present U.S. economy have also made the old warning signposts of impending inflation less reliable.[20] At one time it was possible to tell when inflation was coming just by watching for a rapid growth in the money supply. Today, with money being exchanged freely between money market and stock funds and bank CDs, it is becoming difficult to know just what the money supply categories really mean. Corporations are now borrowing more from sources such as financial companies that are more difficult to track. Price messages often deliver mixed or spotty signals: Gold and steel may be up whereas oil or retail prices may simultaneously decline. The heavy weighting of commodity price indexes toward agricultural commodities tells little about the underlying strength of the industrial economy. Measures of industrial materials are also becoming less important as technology and highly skilled workers dominate the economic scene, marking a transition from a labor-based industrialized to a knowledge-based high-tech society and worker. Domestic industrial production and capacity utilization rates may no longer presage shortages and consequent price increases because the expansion of U.S. manufacturing abroad can now cushion against excess domestic demand. And as leaner, restructured companies get more out of both their workers and their machines, factories can meet demand more efficiently to boost profitability.

HOW TO USE *INVESTOR'S BUSINESS DAILY* TO MONITOR INFLATION

It has been easy to translate the prices of goods into measurable indicators. The inflation picture, in a basic way, can be followed by looking at an index of raw materials (commodities), the Producer Price Index, and the Consumer Price Index. To these must be added inflationary pressures exerted by excess factory capacity, growth in wages, foreign competition, and competition among domestic companies to retain market share.

The three main price indexes seem to be logically related to one another. Changes in the prices of raw materials should be expected to affect the production costs of final manufactured products directly, which costs, in turn, would be passed on to the consumer. On occasion, worries about job security have restrained consumers from buying, so that rising commodity prices have not always translated into higher consumer prices. On the reverse end, more consumer demand can bid up consumer prices, thus raising profit margins for manufacturing companies. Knowing that manufacturers are making more profits motivates the suppliers of raw materials to raise their own prices and share in the wealth. However, commodity prices as reflected by the CRB Index have provided a poor, and often misleading, representation of industrial raw materials. As a result, the 12-month rate of change of the Producer Price Index (PPI) and the Consumer Price Index (CPI), monitored on a monthly basis, has become the foundation for tracking inflation.

The PPI and the CPI are reported each month in the *Inside Today* box on the first page of Section A, and as a graph and table with an accompanying commentary in *The Economy* in Section B (Exhibits 4-9 and 4-10). Although the CPI is a broader index that includes the services sector, wholesale prices, as represented in the PPI, should be given due attention, because they often signal commodity price pressures that could work their way down to the consumer over the coming months.

The *PPI* is a variable-weight index that ignores the services industries. Producer prices (wholesale prices) for finished goods are shown for the last decade as a year-over-year percentage change in prices paid by U.S. manufacturers (Exhibit 4-9). The changes in the total price for all finished goods and

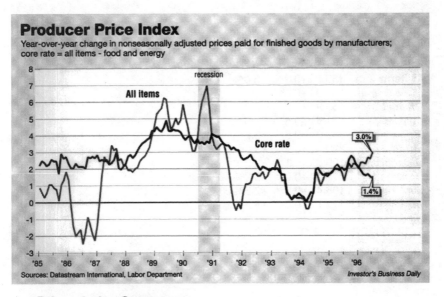

Prices Index Summary

(not seasonally adjusted)	August	July
Finished Goods	**131.9**	**131.5**
Ex. food & energy	141.8	142.0
Consumer goods	130.4	129.9
Consumer foods	135.4	133.6
Intermediate	**126.0**	**125.8**
Foods & feeds	132.3	131.9
Crude	**114.5**	**114.8**
Foods & feeds	129.4	130.4

EXHIBIT 4-9. The Producer Price Index.

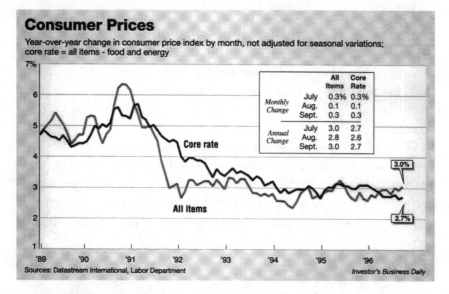

Consumer Prices

Year-over-year change in consumer price index by month, not adjusted for seasonal variations; core rate = all items - food and energy

		All Items	Core Rate
Monthly Change	July	0.3%	0.3%
	Aug.	0.1	0.1
	Sept.	0.3	0.3
Annual Change	July	3.0	2.7
	Aug.	2.8	2.6
	Sept.	3.0	2.7

Sources: Datastream International, Labor Department

Investor's Business Daily

CPI Summary

	Index[1]	Sept./Aug.[2]	'96/'95[3]
All items	157.8	+0.3%	+3.0%
Food & drinks	155.0	+0.5	+3.7
Housing	153.9	+0.2	+2.9
Apparel	131.5	+0.5	-0.9
Transportation	143.2	+0.5	+3.2
Medical care	229.4	+0.2	+3.3
Entertainment	159.8	+0.1	+3.2
Other	218.3	+0.0	+3.9%
Core rate	166.4	+0.3%	+2.7%
Energy	111.7	+0.0	+5.2
Food	155.0	+0.5	+3.8

[1,3] not seasonally adjusted

[2] seasonally adjusted

EXHIBIT 4-10.   The Consumer Price Index.

the changes in the core rate of inflation (excluding food and energy) are compared. Since prices paid for finished goods must be put in perspective with prices and supplies bought earlier in the production process, an accompanying table also gives the most recent monthly percentage change, and the change over the same month of the previous year, for the categories of finished goods, intermediate goods, and crude goods.

In each category, the total plus the core rate of change (excluding food and energy) are shown. It is the 12-month percentage change that allows the annual rate of inflation at the wholesale level to be calculated.

The *CPI* is reported each month after the PPI. It includes fewer items than the PPI and is a fixed-weight index requiring few revisions. Consumer prices (shop prices) for services and goods are shown for the last decade as a year-over-year percentage change in prices paid by consumers to U.S. retailers (Exhibit 4-10). It is the 12-month percentage change that allows the annual rate of inflation at the retail level to be calculated. Long-term price stability has been generally assumed when the average annual CPI increase has been 2 percent or less. The table also breaks down the components of the market basket in terms of the prices for food and beverages plus oil and energy prices (core rate), and prices for meals, housing, apparel, transportation, medical care, entertainment, and others. The CPI must also be interpreted within the context of other consumer-related statistics, especially real earnings and the other measures of inflation, and it is such correlations that are put into perspective in an accompanying commentary.

The PPI tends to reach peaks and bottoms before the CPI, and the PPI is more volatile than the CPI. Although producer and consumer inflation rates generally track together, consumer inflation rates have been more closely tied to changes in general interest rates. The difference between a corporation's costs of production (PPI) and what it charges customers (CPI) has been advocated as a proxy for corporate profit margins, and therefore as a predictor of stock prices over the next 1 to 3 years.[21] The greater the gap of CPI minus PPI, the better the stock market action over the next 12 months. On the other hand, when PPI has exceeded CPI by at least 5 percentage points, indicating negative corporate margins, the stock market as measured by the S&P 400 has declined.[22]

Turn to the *Futures* section of the newspaper from the Contents. The *CRB Index* can be located in a small chart called *Futures Prices* at the top of a page of the *Futures* section (Exhibit 4-8). This chart lists the high, low, and close

(CL) prices and the year-to-date percentage change (*since Jan 1*). The graph tracks the weekly closing prices over the past 18 months. The CL figure should be the one to monitor. The commodity "quotes" page also provides 6-month charts every day on 18 different futures markets which give an overall view of how some of the individual components of the CRB are doing, and they show the progress of the financial and currency markets.

The *Employment Cost Index* is reported quarterly and reflects the previous quarter. The data are presented graphically as a seasonally adjusted, year-over-year percentage rate of change over a period of 10 years. Besides the employment cost of all private industries, the data are broken down into the services and manufacturing sectors. The index should be linked to production (PPI) and to the productivity data and the unemployment rate: A fall in unemployment below 6 percent is usually the stage when pressures traditionally start to build upon unit labor costs.

NOTES

1. John Kenneth Galbraith, *Economics in Perspective* (Houghton Miflin, Boston, 1987).

2. Donald Nichols, *Investing in Uncertain Times* (Longman Financial Services, NY, 1988).

3. Robert Carson, *What Economists Know* (St. Martin's Press, NY, 1990).

4. Further information on the business cycle can be obtained from the writings of Wesley Mitchell, especially his classic *Business Cycles and Their Causes* (University of California Press, Berkeley, 1913; reprinted 1941), and the writings of Geoffrey Moore, particularly the collection of his papers compiled in *Business Cycles, Inflation, and Forecasting* (National Bureau of Economic Research Studies in the Business Cycles, No. 24, Ballinger Publishing, Cambridge, MA, 1983). A recent comprehensive monograph is that by Howard Sherman, *The Business Cycle* (Princeton University Press, NJ, 1991). See also Nichols, *Investing in Uncertain Times*.

5. Wesley Mitchell, *Business Cycles: The Problem and Its Setting* (National Bureau of Economic Research, NY, 1927).

6. Robert Heilbroner and Lester Thurow, *Economics Explained* (Simon & Schuster, NY, 1987). The distinction between nominal and real GDP is well explained in this book, from which this and the following paragraphs are adapted.

7. *Ibid.*

8. *Ibid.*

9. This section is put together from the ideas discussed in Robert Bowker, *Strategic Market Timing* (New York Institute of Finance [NYIF], NY, 1989), in which the strategies described here are developed in detail. See also Nichols, *Investing in Uncertain Times.*

10. Nichols, *Investing in Uncertain Times.* This paragraph is put together from the words and ideas in Nichols' book.

11. Stansbury W. Carnes and Stephen D. Slifer, *The Atlas of Economic Indicators* (HarperBusiness, NY, 1991).

12. Board of Governors of the Federal Reserve System, *The Federal Reserve System, Purposes and Function* (Washington, DC, 1963).

13. *Ibid.*

14. David Jones, *The Politics of Money* (New York Institute of Finance, NY, 1991). An experienced Fed watcher discusses the techniques of the trade, revealing the money management goals and indicators followed by the Fed under Greenspan.

15. David Jones, *Fed Watching and Interest Rate Projections* (New York Institute of Finance, NY, 1989). This paragraph has been put together from the discussions in the two books on the Fed by David Jones.

16. Jones, *Fed Watching and Interest Rate Projections.*

17. Lawrence Stein, *Value Investing* (John Wiley & Sons, NY, 1987).

18. This section is put together from a variety of sources, the primary of which are Norman Frumkin's two books: *Tracking America's Economy* (M. E. Sharpe, Armonk, NY, 1992) and *Guide to Economic Indicators* (M. E. Sharpe, Armonk, NY, 1990). Other sources are Edmund Mennis, *How the Economy Works* (New York Institute of Finance, NY, 1991); Carnes and Slifer, *Atlas of Economic Indicators*; and Alfred Malabre, Jr.,

Understanding the New Economy (Dow Jones Irwin, Homewood, IL, 1989).

19. Stephen Leeb, *Market Timing for the Nineties* (HarperBusiness, NY, 1993).

20. Howard Gleckman, commentary, *Business Week*, February 21, 1994, p. 86. This paragraph is put together from Gleckman's commentary.

21. Leeb, *Market Timing for the Nineties.*

22. *Ibid.*

THE PSYCHOLOGY OF MARKET BEHAVIOR[1]

In the modern world, the authority of psychology has rivaled the authority of mathematics. It has become one of the inescapable truths of the marketplace that acute stock price movements are predominantly determined by psychological attitudes to fundamental factors.[2] The price of a stock at any given time is essentially a bet on what the price will be sometime in the future, and both buyer and seller have an emotional stake in being right.[3] A stock's short-term performance has very little to do with corporate developments, except insofar as the strength of its balance sheet creates a group of people willing and anxious to buy the stock.[4] Much more has been determined by the plurality of motivations, whether they be a vulgar greed or fear, or a naive hope or ambition, or a more cloaked self-interest.

Sentiment analysis seeks to understand these *people* that play the money game, because what the players think often matters more than what the true facts may be. Here is a very different, purely psychological, type of influence on stock prices. Little has usually changed in the underlying intrinsic values, but something in the outside corporate or economic world dictates that stock prices be revalued, and different sectors of the financial community begin looking upon the same circumstances from a different viewpoint than before. As a result of this changed way of appraising the same set of basic facts, a changed appraisal is made of the price that people are willing to pay for the same shares.

Sentiment has been described as a gossamer thing; it is hard enough to measure day by day, let alone to reconstruct from times past, and sentiment indicators, in general, have been the toughest set of indicators to use.[5] The market rolls along in an ebb and flow of mass psychological cycles: panic followed by distrust, relief, cautious acceptance, and then optimism; then enthusiasm, euphoria, and an overwhelming certainty that everything is going to be wonderful forever; sliding off, once again, into concern, desperation, and back to panic.[6] It is in the transition of the crowd from not believing to believing, from pessimism to optimism, that the real money has been made; it takes a change in sentiment to turn cash into a demand for stocks. Maximum profits have been gleaned when the crowd has been either joyous or despairing, because people's greatest dreams and worst fears are in fact never fully realized.[7] And price behavior and volume behavior on the charts may not necessarily equal people's sentiment behavior.

The investing crowd today may be different—represented by the eager performance-oriented managers of mutual funds, banks, and pension plans—but human nature is still the same. Understanding personal intuition, and sensing patterns of sentiment behavior, is still as vital an aspect of the investment process as before, and no easier. The psychology exhibited by investors bears a close relation to that studied by psychologists. Psychologists have explained the influence of emotion by comparing it to instinct. The instinct for the preservation of wealth is one of the strongest of all motivations and, when threatened, has caused individuals to react in certain senseless and inexplicable ways.

It has been asserted that there are instincts, rather base ones, present in individuals that come to the surface only when they are in a crowd.[8] The most striking characteristic of a crowd, whoever the individuals are that compose it, is that the sense of responsibility which controls individuals disappears entirely when they form a crowd.[9] The transformation of individuals into a crowd puts them in a sort of collective mind, a communication of feeling not easy to explain, which makes them feel and act in a manner quite different from that of each individual. The sentiments and ideas of all people in a gathering take one and the same direction. There is an unwillingness to be out of step. Any display of premeditation by crowds is out of the question. An individual in a crowd acquires, just from being in the crowd, a sentiment of suggestibility which allows him or her to yield to different instincts that often lead to acts of irresistible impetuosity.

The lessons of history have shown that crowds have been powerful only for destruction. Civilizations have been created and directed only by a small intellectual aristocracy, not as yet by crowds.[10] The process of civilization, like the process of investing, has involved rules and discipline, a passing from the instinctive to the rational state with a forethought for the future, all of which conditions a crowd is incapable of realizing. It is not necessary that a crowd should be numerous. A few young and powerful money managers gathered together can constitute a crowd, and even though they may be distinguished people of learning, they can assume all the characteristics of a crowd. Fortunately, though the wishes of crowds may be frenzied, they are not durable. Crowds have been incapable of functioning for any length of time.

The strongest crowd sentiments in the financial markets have been those of greed and fear: the fear of losing everything, and the greed to double or triple it. The wave of greed begins in rising markets, and it is probably greed that forms the tops of bull markets. Why else, it has been asked, would one buy into a climax? And sufficient people do so, and merge into the crowd, to produce a market top.[11] The same thing happens in reverse out of fear. When prices start to fall, it is again that unconscious, senseless impulse to be part of the crowd that causes faith to evaporate completely, and one is swept into a mob psychology of panic and fear that sells into a market bottom. Good news, bad news, friends, and strangers all conspire to influence crowd behavior in the financial markets. Being consistently right in the market has often had to be a lonely job.

THE SUBSTRATE OF MARKET SENTIMENT INDICATORS

Market sentiment indicators are ways to measure the sentiment of the investing crowd. They either have consisted of market polls to evaluate the bullish or bearish condition of the participants being questioned or have measured market transactions of the general public or of selected market professionals who make their living from trading.

Primary among the market professionals are the specialists who work on the floor of the exchange and act as its leaders. It is the *specialist* who determines the price of his specialty stock within the perimeters of existing supply and demand. A specialist is a broker's broker, since all orders for buying or selling his specialty stocks must go through him. Regular brokers bring to him the orders of their customers who wish to buy or sell shares in his stocks. Another group of market professionals are the exchange *members* who have purchased a "seat" on the exchange which allows them to trade directly for themselves, or for their company, without paying commissions. Like the specialists, the exchange members are expected to show good insight into what is going on, and member activity has also been regarded as reflecting the sentiments of the market professional and the true condition of the market.

In contrast to the professionals are the market nonprofessionals or the general public, the many ordinary investors whose transactions, by virtue of their limited money, have frequently involved fewer than a 100 shares of stock, called the *odd lot*. An odd lot is any transaction on the NYSE amounting to under 100 shares (which is called a round lot). Since it is presumed that market professionals do not deal in small blocks of securities, odd lots reflect the activity of small investors. They provide a clue to the opinion of the investing public, and they form a structure for measuring extremes of public optimism or pessimism which have usually marked the turning points of market movements.

The conventional teaching has been that odd lotters tend to buy and sell at the wrong times, and odd-lot activity, tracked by the odd-lot statistics, represents a contrary signal of true market sentiment. Thus, odd-lot buying is a bearish signal and odd-lot selling is bullish. In recent years, the reliability of odd-lot statistics has diminished substantially, possibly even destroyed beyond repair, partly because the nonprofessional investor has indeed become more knowledgeable, but mainly because the introduction of options trading has allowed odd lotters, with their scant cash resources, to meet their goals by buying low-priced options. Options have become another way of duplicating the speculative excitement of low-priced stocks.

The advent of options trading has produced additional sentiment indicators to take the place of the odd-lot statistics. An *option* is a contract between two parties which gives the owner of the contract the right to buy or sell a specific amount of an underlying security at a specified price and by a specified time. The price specified in the option contract is called the *strike* price, and the specified time is the expiration date on the contract. For most options, expiration falls on the Saturday following the third Friday of the month at 11:59 A.M. Eastern time. Contracts can be written for periods of 30 days, 60 days, 90 days, 6 months, and, rarely, 1 year. The person purchasing the contract is called the option buyer; the buyer is the only one who can exercise the option. The person selling the contract to the buyer is called the option writer; the writer is obligated to fulfill the terms of the contract when the buyer elects to exercise the option. The buyer can exercise the option at any time during the term of the contract before the expiration date.

An option contract that gives the buyer the right to purchase the underlying security is called a *call option,* and one that gives the buyer the right to sell the underlying security, under the terms of the option contract, is called a *put option.* A call is purchased if the buyer believes that the market value of the underlying security is going to rise in the future, and a put is purchased if the underlying security is expected to drop in value. The amount that the buyer pays to the option writer for the contract is called the *premium.* The premium is the market price of the option, and it fluctuates continually. It is quoted in points, with 1 point equal to $1, so that the total value of an option contract is the premium price multiplied by the number of shares, usually 100, covered by the contract. In the case of market index options, the premium is multiplied by the index multiplier, which is also usually 100.

The utility of the sentiment indicators that are based on options trading stems from the fact that the public is the majority buyer of stock option contracts. Hence, the purchases and sales of options reflect the public's expectations for the direction of movement of a stock or market index. The sellers, or writers, of stock options are the market professionals who are hedging their positions, and are therefore not trading simply on the basis of their market outlook. Heavy call option volume relative to put volume indicates that the public is bullish and, interpreted in a contrarian way, indicates that the stock market is poised for a decline. A bearish public outlook is indicated by more trading volume in put options compared with call options, and such conditions have invariably set the stage for a market rally.

Additional sentiment indicators have arisen from the short-selling activities of the professionals and the public. *Selling short* is a technique that allows one to profit from an expected decline in the price of a stock. Selling short in the market has always been an unequivocal expression of investor pessimism, except when it is done for tax avoidance purposes or to ensure an investor against a decline. Since market professionals have agreed that a bearish "majority" sentiment is a bullish signal for stock prices, a rising interest in short selling by the public is a bullish signal.

It is important to appreciate the implications of short selling. Short sellers *borrow* stock through a broker and sell it immediately at the market price. The sellers now have the cash in hand acquired from the sale. They believe that the stock will decline enough in price in the near future to permit them to buy it back ("cover") at the lower price and return it to the broker. The difference between the higher price at which they sold the stock originally and the lower price paid to acquire the stock again to return it to the broker is their profit. Hence, eventually the short sellers must *buy* the same number of shares to replace what they sold when they first borrowed the stock. Because they have now acted like a bear, they must later behave like a bull.

The very nature of short selling dictates that every past short sale is a future purchase. Therefore, the short interest or short position, which are both terms used to identify the number of shares sold short but not yet replaced, forms a cushion for stock prices. If prices decline, short sellers will *buy* to cash in on their profits. If prices go up, short sellers may rush to *buy* to cut their losses. Hence, it has been proposed that the very nature of short selling, to some extent, dictates that when at any time everybody says the market is going down, it will soon go up. It is bullish to have plenty of bears around!

HOW TO USE *INVESTOR'S BUSINESS DAILY* TO MONITOR MARKET SENTIMENT

Psychological market indicators are presented on the *Market Charts* page in a rectangular box in the top left corner of the large chart of the S&P 500 Index. In this location, they can be viewed along with the three market averages (Exhibit 5-1). The current value is **boldfaced,** and the high and low values over the past 12 months and 5 years are shown for each indicator, together with the dates when the high and low values were recorded. Since a change in trend is more useful than the actual value, some of the indicators are displayed, in turn on different days, as a graph on the top of the page. This graph presents the weekly change in trend over the previous 6 months. The horizontal axis scale on this graph is similar to that of the general market indicators shown on the page, thus allowing easy comparison of the trend of a sentiment indicator with that of the market indexes.

The first indicator listed in the box is the percentage of *investment advisers* who are bullish or bearish (Exhibit 5-1). Stock market investment advisers, though considered to be well informed and therefore most likely to offer quality advice,

PSYCHOLOGICAL MARKET INDICATORS	Current	5 YEAR High	Date	Low	Date	12 MONTH High	Date	Low	Date
1. % Investment Advisors Bearish (50% = Bullish; 20% = Bearish)	36.0%	59.1%	(12/12/94)	19.1%	1/21/92	44.0%	9/ 2/96	28.6%	1/15/96
% Invest. Advisors Bullish(35% Bullish; 55% Bearish) – Investor's Intelligence	46.5%	60.0%	1/21/92	23.3%	7/11/94	55.4%	2/26/96	33.1%	11/ 7/95
2. Odd Lot Short Sales/Odd Lot Sales	4.71%	26.6%	6/ 1/92	0.35%	6/16/92	21.3%	3/12/96	1.96%	12/25/95
3. Public/NYSE Specialist Short Sales (above 0.6 Bullish; below 0.35 Bearish)	1.41	2.25	6/14/96	0.51	2/ 7/92	2.25	6/14/96	1.07	11/10/95
4. Short Interest Ratio (NYSE Short Interest/Avg Daily Volume prior 30 days)	5.99	7.20	9/ 6/96	3.13	2/21/92	7.20	9/ 6/96	4.12	12/19/95
5. Ratio of price premiums in Puts versus Calls	0.71	2.08	7/ 7/95	0.29	7/15/96	1.38	5/13/96	0.29	7/15/96
6. Ratio of Trading Volume in Puts versus Calls	0.58	1.23	1/24/92	0.41	9/20/96	1.06	7/16/96	0.41	9/20/96
7. Mutual Fund Share Purchases/Redemptions (X – Money Market Funds)	1.75	2.82	2/ 2/93	0.98	11/30/94	2.21	12/29/95	1.00	11/ 2/95
8. AMEX Daily Trading Volume as % of NYSE Daily Volume	4.36%	7.63%	10/ 7/96	1.00%	9/ 4/92	7.63%	10/ 7/96	3.37%	10/16/96
9. OTC Daily Trading Volume as % of NYSE Daily Volume	109%	196%	5/ 7/96	59.4%	12/20/91	196%	5/ 7/96	89.0%	12/15/95
10. Number of Stock Splits in Investor's Business Daily 6000 (prior 30 days)	77	169	6/21/96	37	11/13/92	169	6/21/96	57	9/12/96
11. New Issues in Last Year as % of All Stocks on NYSE	31.6%	33.9%	3/ 4/94	16.0%	11/ 5/91	31.9%	11/ 1/96	19.9%	11/ 2/95
12. Price – to – Book Value of Dow Jones Industrial Average	4.42	4.45	(10/18/96)	2.61	2/17/93	4.45	10/18/96	3.68	10/18/96
13. Price to Earnings Ratio of Dow Jones Industrial Average	18.9	40.6	6/15/92	13.7	10/26/95	19.0	10/18/96	14.0	11/ 7/95
14. Current Dividend Yield of Dow Jones Industrial Average	2.18%	3.33%	(10/ 9/92	2.11%	3/ 5/96)	2.40%	3/ 5/96	2.11%	3/ 5/96

Investor's Business Daily 6000 Accumulation/Distribution totals($5 stocks and above)
A 1,621 – 29, B 3,013 + 30, C 1,288 – 14, D 852 – 8, E 275 + 6.

EXHIBIT 5-1. Market Sentiment Indicators.

tend to be trend followers. They have, for this reason, become a good proxy for the "majority" opinion and contrarian thinking. They tend to turn bullish after prices have started to rise and remain bullish, with some notable exceptions, even at stock market peaks. Conversely, when a market has been declining, advisers tend to get overly pessimistic right into a major bottom. This index is commonly used in a contrarian fashion to analyze the nature of bullish sentiment over the forthcoming 6- to 12-month time spans.[12]

Since 1963, *Investor's Intelligence*, an advisory service, has been compiling data on the opinions of about 120 publishers of market letters and has calculated a *sentiment index*. Some have called it the "bulls over bulls plus bears" indicator, and it represents the percentage of bullish market letter writers ("bulls") in relation to the total of all advisers ("bulls plus bears") expressing an opinion on the market. The latest *Investor's Intelligence* data appear in the Thursday edition of *Investor's Business Daily*. A criticism of the investment advisory services indicator has been the delay involved between the reading of market letters and the weighing of their content to the actual publishing of the results.

Whenever the indicator has moved below the 35 percent level and then moved up above it, an important buy signal has been generated. This has usually been followed by market rises. Bear markets have touched bottom when 60 percent or more of advisory services have turned outright bearish: The indicator was 62 percent bearish when the market was bottoming in 1982. A bear market rally may be impending when bullish advisers fall below 40 percent and the bears rise above 30 percent.

Bull market peaks have normally been associated with over 60 percent of advisers being bullish before a big market turn. When the percentage of bears falls below 15 and the percentage of bulls rises above 65, the stock market is near an important top.[13] It has performed well on the bearish side in a bull market. When bullish advisers rise to more than 54 percent and bears fall below 20 percent, a drop in the market may be expected. The indicators have been particularly accurate when one or both numbers have shown a sudden change following a period of 5 to 6 weeks in a volatile market. Ten-week moving-average readings of bearish opinions below 20 percent indicate probable market bottoms, while readings over 50 percent suggest a market top.[14] Some have proposed a 13-week moving average with a reading of less than 40 percent being bullish and more than 70 percent being bearish.[15]

The next two indicators shown in the box (2 and 3) relate to short-selling statistics. The *odd-lot short sales ratio* reflects crowd psychology; a value above 4.0 is a bullish event. The actual number of shares sold short each day in lots of less than 100 is first determined. Dividing the odd-lot short sales by the total odd-lot sales (including short sales) gives the odd-lot short sale ratio. Lower prices tempt the small stockholder to buy and the short seller to sell. Higher prices do the opposite. Odd lotters are generally late to short during major declines, and hence their short selling has reached peaks at bear market lows.

Readings over 1 percent on a daily basis are favorable, but a ratio over 2 percent (and as high as 6 percent) has been necessary to call a market bottom and signal a buying opportunity. Relatively high readings that persist as the market is rising indicate a continuing comfortable buying climate. Hence this ratio has moved in an opposite direction to the DJIA. When many stocks are selling at low prices in a general market decline and odd-lot short selling continues to be strong, the indicator should be regarded as being even more bullish. Ultrahigh readings have heralded the end of bear markets. When odd-lot short sales divided by all odd-lot sales amount to more than 0.05 over a 5-day period, it can be assumed that the end of the bear market is near. The odd-lot short sales ratio works effectively only at market bottoms; at market tops, readings of less than 1 percent have been bearish but often with long lead times.

Specialist short-selling activity is tracked by *public/NYSE specialist short selling;* when the indicator is above 0.6, the market is likely to move higher. A value below 0.35 has indicated an imminent market decline. A low reading indicates a reluctance by the public to go short in anticipation of further market advances and, since this is the majority (public) view, the traditional interpretation has been to take a contrary position. Hence, when public sentiment is bullish, professional opinion is bearish, and vice versa.

The next group of four indicators reflect, in varying ways, the sentiments of public investors as they participate either in short selling or in the options markets, or in the equity mutual funds. In addition to the short sales and odd-lot ratios shown here, the odd-lot figures themselves are reported separately in *Investor's Business Daily* every day, a day later.

Short interest ratio (4 in the box) represents total short-interest activity in the market relative to total market volume over the same period. High short interest means a high future demand for the stock and is a potentially bullish sign. Interpreted in this way on a contrary basis, the ratio is most bullish for the market when it reads 1.8 or higher, and even more bullish when the reading exceeds 2.0—that is, a short interest of twice the average daily volume.[16] When the short-interest ratio falls below 1.5 percent, a bearish signal is generated. The value of a buy signal can be enhanced when interpreted in the context of the market milieu—a bullish signal after a lengthy market decline is more significant than a similar signal occurring after a market has already been rising. The actual amount of short interest is of less value than the ratio and its trend.

The next two indicators (5 and 6 in the box) examine the sentiments of the options traders in terms of the *options premium ratio* and the *put/call volume ratio*. It has been pointed out that 4 consecutive days of very low put/call volume ratios have invariably led to marked declines in the DJIA, whereas 6 or 7 consecutive days of very high ratios have led to a rally in the Dow. Eight consecutive days of put/call volume ratios of more than 0.63 were recorded only three times in the last 12 years, and in each case the DJIA showed a significant bull rally about a week later.[17] The daily values for the options premium ratio since 1986 have ranged between 0.03 and 1.74. The median value for the ratio has been in the low to mid 0.60s. The market almost always makes its bottoms at option premium ratio values of 0.51 and under.[18] It almost always forms its tops at values of 0.7 and over unless the values exceed 1.16. At values over 1.16, the market either flattens or continues to rally until the values return to the 0.70 to 1.16 range.

The next indicator (7) examines the sentiments of mutual fund investors and managers. This is a difficult indicator to use. The *Mutual Fund Purchases/Redemptions Index* is a ratio that compares the cash reserves, used as a proxy for institutional buying power, with the redemptions over the previous 3 months. The ratio has been used as an indicator of how much purchasing power portfolio managers have. The theory is that when fund purchases are high relative to redemptions, the funds are taking in additional cash to buy stocks and bonds. Conversely, when the ratio is low, managers are closer to the point of having to sell holdings to meet redemptions.

The redemptions mirror the selling pressures exerted on the market by the public. Low redemptions (leading to a rise in the index value) have traditionally reflected public optimism and therefore, in a contrarian way, a bearish condition. At the same time, low redemptions have provided more cash on hand and more buying power to the fund managers who can buy more in the market, thus driving up prices. Put another way, when the ratio becomes higher, the market should also move higher because the funds will have additional cash to buy stocks.[19] The 5-year range of the ratio has been roughly between 1 and 3. A high ratio of mutual fund share purchases to redemptions, indicating a surplus of cash available to fund managers to buy stocks, usually leads to higher market moves. A record high value of 4.63 in 1985 set off a 41 percent gain in the DJIA over the following 11 months.[20] Conversely, when the ratio is low, indicating drainage of cash, market prices are likely to go down. The ratio may be used as a contrarian indicator in bear markets: When redemptions are at their high during market lows, one should be considering purchases.

The next group of four sentiment indicators in the box (8 to 11) reflects the intensity of speculative activity in the markets. The higher the degree of speculation, the higher the volume of trading on the Amex and OTC markets, and the greater the number of stock splits and the sale of new and secondary issues. Comparison of trading volumes between the NYSE and the OTC markets has been conventionally used as an indicator of investor speculation. Higher *OTC/NYSE volume ratios* occur when trading volume in small and speculative OTC stocks is greater than that in the more solid companies on the NYSE. The first time that OTC volume exceeded that on the NYSE was in 1983. Since then, this ratio has served as a bearish indicator, because spikes in its value have coincided with several market tops over the last decade (e.g., mid-1983, mid-1987, and spring of 1991). Conversely, abnormally low levels have been noted on the eve of bull markets (as in July 1982). When speculation is running high, it usually signals that the stock market is approaching a top. Conversely, when speculation is low, a market bottom may be imminent. This ratio is therefore considered to be a contrarian indicator, because as trading becomes more speculative, it is usually time to become more cautious.

The more bullish investors are, the more money they invest. But as more money is invested, less is available for the further buying required to push the market even higher. Some believe that it is speculative institutional buying which tends to chase rallies in any market, leading to a rise in OTC volume. Others feel that the higher volume is a result of the public getting into the market late in the cycle and creating much of the same effect. Associated increases in initial public offerings (IPOs) and a more frenzied buying of new issues confirm the atmosphere of heightened speculation.

A speculation model has been constructed by plotting the 10-day simple moving average of each of the daily NYSE, Amex, and Nasdaq composite volumes. If the Nasdaq reading is over 85 percent of the NYSE and the Amex is reading over 14 percent of the NYSE, then both figures mean that the markets are experiencing too much speculative buying and a short-term reversal will soon take place. In the most recent years, however, there has been no consistent pattern to confirm that heavy OTC trading has indeed heralded a downturn in the overall market. For example, from November 5 to November 27, 1991, OTC volume consistently ran ahead of NYSE volume. Yet in the following 3 months, the Dow advanced 12.7 percent and the Nasdaq moved up 21.3 percent. On the other hand, the ratio reached a high of 1.21 to 1 in late 1993, preceding a 9 percent decline in the S&P 500 in early 1994.

The last three items in the box (12 to 14) allow a historical valuation of the market to identify overbought or oversold conditions of the market averages as a whole (Exhibit 5-1). (See the discussion in Chapter 6.) Price-to-book, price-to-earnings, and dividend yield ratios of the Dow Jones Industrials can help determine if the market is fairly valued. They can reveal when market risks are probably low, and when they are probably high.

The question of valuation is an important one, because periods of extreme valuation determine the proper time for making adjustments among assets in a portfolio. When valuation indicators are neutral, as they should be most of the time, no action is necessary. Low dividend yields and high P/E or price-to-book values imply high and generally overvalued stock prices and have invariably been followed by broad declines in market prices. Conversely, high dividend yields and low P/E or price-to-book ratios indicate undervalued conditions with a prospect of generally rising prices. Similar ratios for individual stocks may be compared with those of the Dow or the S&P 500 to gauge the relative performance of a stock to the overall market in terms of an overbought or oversold condition.

Extreme low points of valuation become identified when market price is 80 percent to 90 percent of book value, and overvaluation occurs at twice book value. Dividend yields are highest during periods of low stock prices, because dividend payments are less volatile than stock prices. When stock prices drop, corporations maintain dividends to sustain investor confidence, thus driving up the dividend yield. It has been shown that when the dividend yield of the broad market (S&P 500) is more than 5.2 percent, the stock market has been cheap and has presented a buying opportunity. A low dividend yield below 3.4 percent has been a signal to sell, since the overvalued market would be susceptible to a decline.[21] It is instructive to note that although low P/E ratios typically prevail during periods of low stock prices, corporate profits fell so low in the early 1930s that even the extremely depressed stock prices of this era returned a very high P/E.

The absolute values of the Dow earnings yield and dividend yield figures are less useful by themselves than when they are interpreted relative to interest rates and the yields on bonds. It is as an instrument of comparative valuation between stocks and fixed-income securities that these market valuation indicators have shown their greatest merit by allowing money to be directed to the investment that shows the best return relative to risk.

NOTES

1. Market technical analysis and market sentiment analysis go together, and therefore most books on technical analysis have good discussions on sentiment analysis. The generally accepted reference books on technical analysis are Martin Pring, *Technical Analysis Explained* (McGraw-Hill, NY, 1991); and Robert Edwards and John Magee, *Technical Analysis of Stock Trends* (1948; new edition NYIF, NY, 1992). Excellent discussions on market psychology are also present in Alexander Elder, *Trading for a Living* (John Wiley & Sons, NY, 1993); the two books by Victor Sperandeo, *Trader Vic: Methods of a Wall Street Master* and *Trader Vic II: Principles of Professional Speculation* (both published by John Wiley & Sons, NY, 1991); and the many articles by Arthur Merrill that have appeared in *Technical Analysis of Stocks and Commodities*. Good discussions of the sentiment indicators by Justin Mamis are scattered throughout the trilogy: *How to Buy* (Farrar, Straus, Giroux, NY, 1982), *When to Sell*, with Robert Mamis (Simon & Schuster, NY, 1977), and *The Nature of Risk* (Addison-Wesley, NY, 1992). See also Investor's Business Daily, *Guide to High-Performance Investing* (O'Neil Data Systems Inc., Los Angeles, 1993); Norman Fosback, *Stock Market Logic* (Financial Publishing

Company, Dearborn, MI, 1976; reprinted 1992); and Gerald Appel, *Winning Stock Market Systems* (Signalert Corp., Great Neck, NY, 1974).

2. Pring, *Technical Analysis Explained.*

3. Mamis and Mamis, *When to Sell.*

4. *Ibid.*

5. *Ibid.*

6. Kenneth Fisher, *Super Stocks* (Dow Jones-Irwin, Homewood, IL,1984).

7. James Grant, *Minding Mr. Market* (Farrar, Straus, Giroux, NY, 1993).

8. Gustave Le Bon, *The Crowd* (1895, Ballantine Books, NY, reprinted 1969). This book is a classic on crowd psychology. This paragraph and the following one are based on Le Bon's book.

9. *Ibid.*

10. *Ibid.*

11. Mamis, *Nature of Risk.*

12. Robert Colby and Thomas Meyers, *The Encyclopedia of Technical Market Indicators* (Dow Jones Irwin, Homewood, IL, 1988).

13. Elder, *Trading for a Living.*

14. Lawrence Stein, *Value Investing* (John Wiley & Sons, NY, 1987).

15. Joe Duarte, "Combining Sentiment Indicators for Timing Mutual Funds," *Technical Analysis of Stocks and Commodities,* January 1992.

16. *Ibid.*

17. Christopher Cadbury, "The Option Premium Ratio," *Technical Analysis of Stocks and Commodities,* July 1994. This section is based upon Cadbury's article.

18. Christopher Cadbury, letter, *Technical Analysis of Stocks and Commodities,* March 1995.

19. *Ibid.*

20. *Ibid.*

21. Stein, *Value Investing.*

THE FUNDAMENTAL VALUES OF CORPORATIONS[1]

It has been said that it is the mission of the sage or the philosopher to judge the value of things and to order them according to their merit. So it has been in the investment universe with the fundamentalist, whose organizing principle dictates making judgments on intrinsic corporate values antecedent to stock purchase. Fundamental analysis is the process of determining the intrinsic value and, therefore, the investment potential of a company on the basis of the company's primary business and the way it is managed. The fundamental analyst is a critic of the behavior of a company, of the performance of its products or services, and of the precision of its balance sheets.

Fundamental analysis is not stock or market analysis but corporation analysis, and this distinction between a corporation and its stock has been a necessary one. Fundamental analysis distinguishes between a quality company and a quality stock. The spell of the stock market today has made the typical investors more dependent on the course of price quotations, and less free to consider themselves as business owners. Some worthy fundamentalists have claimed that, if the markets were to cease trading completely, they would come out just as well without a market and the vagaries of its cycles.[2] Herein lies the keen difference between a corporation and its common stock, which, traded by the market masters and mobs that play the money game, may acquire vicarious qualities independent of the properties of the corporation that it represents.

CORPORATE EARNINGS

Earnings have been *the* fundamental factor in determining the fair price of shares. They are the fuel that propels the U.S. stock market, and American companies have learned to focus relentlessly on earnings and react swiftly to market shifts. Every corporation strives to keep its quarterly earnings up, or else its share price goes down as investors bail out. Projected earnings estimates are educated opinions, but they have gained importance because they are a numerical view of expectations, and changing expectations have influenced stock prices.

Earnings, also called *profits,* are the net income of a corporation after all expenses including depreciation, interest, and taxes have been paid. *Earnings per share* (EPS) are obtained by dividing a company's total after-tax earnings (profits) by the company's number of common shares outstanding. It is a direct measure of the company's effective use of equity. Total earnings of a corporation are of less relevance than its earnings per share: A company may show dramatic growth in total corporate earnings, yet if its working-capital needs have been financed through the sale of more equity (common stock), thus creating a larger number of shares outstanding, earnings per share may actually decline.

Annual earnings over past years and current quarterly earnings both need to be examined. Any company whose earnings have been growing consistently and, more important, are likely to continue to grow consistently has something unique about it. Extraordinary one-time gains in earnings should be ignored. It has been shown that between 1970 and 1982, the average annual compounded growth rate in earnings of those stocks that had the greatest price movements was 24 percent, *before* they began their price rise.[3] The median, or most common, growth rate was 21 percent.[4] Thus, the annual compounded growth rate of earnings of companies whose stocks have been worth buying has ranged from 20 percent to 50 percent, or even more. Moreover, each year's annual earnings per share during the last 5 years should also be higher than the prior year's earnings. One year of low earnings in the last 5 may be acceptable as long as the following year's earnings have recovered quickly and have returned to new highs.[5] The strength of a company's EPS over the past 5 years, and its EPS performance over the previous two quarters, has been used by *Investor's Business Daily* to form a unique EPS ranking system for all stocks (see Chapter 2).

LIMITATIONS OF EARNINGS

Earnings can be subject to engaging accounting practices such as depreciation and inventory adjustments.[6] Since depreciation is essentially a deduction from reported income, the less the depreciation, the more the earnings. Conversely, the greater the depreciation, the less the net income reported on the income sheet. Moreover, higher earnings can be bought through prudent acquisitions or even borrowed.

If the reliability of actual reported earnings, both past and current, is often considered uncertain, the methods of predicting the future value of a company through projected earnings are plagued by even more ambiguities. Most investment institutions produce earnings forecasts for the companies that they are following. Because analysts exchange information and follow a crowd mentality by producing duplicative research reports, earnings estimates tend to move in trends. A significant number of identical forecasts can be highly persuasive!

It has been shown that the mean error made by analysts in forecasting projected earnings for periods of 1 year or less is 16.6 percent.[7] Earnings projections since 1973 for the 30 DJIA stocks have had an average margin of error of 47.9 percent per year when predicted earnings were compared with those actually reported a year later.[8] In a recent study by Zacks Investment Research, a Chicago firm, forecasts of annual earnings versus actual earnings for 399 companies over an 11-year period ending in 1992 showed that, in the first month of a fiscal year, analysts' forecasts averaged 57 percent too high. Revisions throughout the year brought analysts closer to reality, but they were still high by 12 percent by the year's end.

Smaller errors are found with estimates of *operating* earnings, which ignore unusual events. When analysts' forecasts have been poor in one year, they have generally been followed by a poor forecast in the following year. Despite the difficulties in formulating a prediction of earnings, it is still desirable and necessary to have a forecast—because it is impossible to determine the intrinsic value of a stock without an estimate of future earnings and dividends. Some market professionals have proposed that, when making such calculations, the consensus forecasts of earnings should be deflated by 10 percent to 15 percent.

HOW TO USE *INVESTOR'S BUSINESS DAILY* TO MONITOR COMPANY EARNINGS

Since earnings are the most significant common denominator for price growth, announcements of a company's current earnings reports are given primary importance in *Investor's Business Daily* each business day. Earnings that are especially remarkable are prominently noted in the *Executive News Summary* section on the first page, and then further elaborated on another page in separate stories. These stories may explain why a quarter was better or worse than expected, or may provide a forecast for the next quarter.

From the Contents on page 1, locate the pages showing the *NYSE Tables, Amex Tables,* and *Nasdaq OTC.* The first column in the *Intelligent Tables* shows the proprietary EPS for every company listed (see Exhibit 2-3, Chapter 2). The letter *k* at the far right side of a company in these tables indicates that an earnings report on that company is due to be released within the next 4 weeks. The dash symbol (—) indicates that an earnings release on the company is reported in that day's issue of *Investor's Business Daily* in the *Earnings* section. In addition, the Nasdaq tables include *percentage annual earnings growth, percentage quarterly EPS*, and *annual earnings estimates* (see Exhibit 2-3 and discussion in Chapter 2).

Since reports of earnings appear before the market opens or during the trading day, a stock's price-volume action on that day is usually a reflection of how the market has received the news. Price action during the days prior to release of an earnings report, and on the day of release, can provide vital information on how a stock will perform over the next several months. Price-volume action during the days preceding the report would show whether the price was rising in anticipation of good earnings results. For example, a stock may move up ahead of the news and then sell off on the actual report. At other times, a stock may be propelled 20 percent or 25 percent higher if an anticipated good report is better than expected.[9] If a stock has risen 1.5 to 2 points on the day of an earnings report, it will invariably outperform the market over the next 3 to 6 months.[10] Conversely, when earnings have been significantly below expectations, stocks have fallen in price on the day of the report, and they have invariably underperformed the market over the next one or two quarters.[11]

Companies with good earnings commonly show price increases. Hence, it may become profitable to follow especially closely the price-volume activity of those companies whose earnings reports are scheduled for release within in the next 4 weeks. Such stocks are identified in the *Intelligent Tables* by the letter *k*. A habit of regularly monitoring the price trends of stocks with the *k* notation will serve to alert an investor to new investment opportunities.[12] On the other hand, price declines in anticipation of poor earnings reports could also protect one from large losses.

Now turn to the page on *Earnings* using the Contents. The *Earnings News* section is an excellent place to find new investment ideas every day. Companies that have shown a rise in earnings, especially a big rise, frequently become the new emerging growth companies with outstanding investment potential. These companies are invariably the leaders or newsmakers for that week, and hence have a high probability of being presented in detail in the charts that make up the daily

Stocks in the News section, or in the Friday's *Your Weekend Graphic Review* section.

Current quarterly corporate earnings that have just been released are reported each business day in the *Earnings* section. This section must be examined every day so that *every* report that comes out can be scanned. By the end of a quarter, one would have seen the earnings of about 5000 companies, from which 30 to 50 may get selected for further study. Proprietary data blocks and highlighting techniques allow the individual investor to scan these earnings reports every day in a time-efficient way.

For example, companies that have reported the highest gains or the greatest losses in their most recent earnings report released that day, when compared with the same quarter a year earlier, are highlighted in a data block called *Best Ups* and *Most Downs*, respectively. This table allows the individual investor to scan the data effortlessly to determine which companies are producing the best results and which ones are to be avoided (Exhibit 6-1). This unique method of displaying earnings reports to highlight potential winners makes it easy to scan every company with the highest earnings gains *in just a few minutes* each day.

Earnings and sales go hand in hand. Rising sales volume is the sine qua non for expanding profits in most growth companies. Without sales, business survival is impossible. A company that is not showing sales growth is not a desirable investment. Such a company may be able to artificially maintain earnings by cutting back operations but it will eventually become noncompetitive. For this reason, both earnings and sales are shown for all companies listed in this box.

The most important figures to check are the percentage change in quarterly earnings and the percentage change in quarterly sales from a year earlier. An up or down arrow indicates whether earnings and sales have accelerated or decelerated from the prior quarter. An asterisk (*) is used to highlight those few companies whose current quarterly increases in earnings have exceeded 30 percent on a year-over-year basis *and* whose sales and earnings gains have both accelerated

94 Ups
Median Change +24%

AKZO NOBEL N V ADR		AKZOY 63
Chemicals-Basic		Eps 40 Rel 65
Qtr. Sep 30:	e1996 (OTC)	e1995
Sales +5%	5,488,000,000	5,219,000,000
Net Income	326,000,000	324,000,000
Earn/shr +1%	2.30	2.28
e – Amounts are in guilders.		

ALEXANDERS INC		ALX 71%
Real Estate Operations		Eps 30 Rel 55
Qtr. Sep 30:	1996 (NYSE)	1995
Sales +31%	5,379,000	4,121,000
Net Loss	-630,000	-1,926,000
Avg shares	5,000,850	5,000,850
Earn/shr	-0.13	-0.39

ALLIED CAPITAL ADVISERS		ALLA 6
Finance-Investment Mgmt		Eps 52 Rel 39
Qtr. Sep 30:	1996 (OTC)	1995
Sales +13%	4,382,000	3,889,000
Net Income	807,000	659,000
Avg shares	9,913,000	9,772,000
Earn/shr +14%	0.08	0.07

ALLIED CAPITAL LENDING		ALCL 15%
Finance-Sbic&Commrcl		Eps 55 Rel 66
Qtr. Sep 30:	1996 (OTC)	1995
Net Income	1,778,000	1,402,000
Avg shares	5,072,000	4,381,000
Earn/shr +9%	0.35	0.32

AMERICA ONLINE INC		AOL 25
Computer-Services		Eps 97 Rel 10
Qtr. Sep 30:	1996 (NYSE)	1995
Sales +77%	349,982,000	197,902,000
Income	19,036,000	d-10,907,000
Extrd loss	e-372,725,000	....
Net Loss	-353,689,000	v-10,907,000
Avg shares	93,169,000	77,147,000
Earn/shr	0.17	d-0.14
Net earn/shr	-3.80	-0.14

d – Loss. e – Writeoff of deferred subscriber acquisition costs. v – Includes $16.9 mil for acquired research and development.

AMTECH CORP		AMTC 6%
Computer-Services		Eps 46 Rel 34
Qtr. Sep 30:	1996 (OTC)	1995
Sales +14%	27,971,000	24,526,000
Net Loss	-63,000	e-422,000
Avg shares	14,622,000	14,666,000
Earn/shr	w....	-0.03

d – Loss. w – Nil. e – Includes $799,000 charge related to acquisition of Cardkey Systems.

Earnings News

The ★ means quarter is up 30% or more & sales & earnings gain accelerated from the prior quarter. ↑ or ↓ means % chg is higher or lower than prior quarter. Stock price, relative strength, group & EPS rank reflect prior day's data.

Best Ups

Company & Symbol		Last Qtr % Chg	Last Qtr Earnings	Last Qtr Sales	A.Tax Margin
MARKWEST HYDROCARBON	MWHX	+180%↑	0.14 vs 0.05	+67%↑	+8.1%↑
F H P INTL CORP	FHPC	+122%	0.40 vs 0.18	+9%	+2.1%
NEWFIELD EXPLORATION CO	NFX	+119%↑	0.46 vs 0.21	+45%↑	+24.2%↑
CHAUVCO RESOURCES LTD	5CHA	+111%↑	0.19 vs 0.09	+7%↑	+16.5%↑
BANNER AEROSPACE INC	BAR	+75%↑	0.07 vs 0.04	+26%↓	+2.0%↑
INFINITY FNCL TECH	INFN	+75%↑	0.07 vs 0.04	+64%↓	+12.2%↑
AMWEST INSURANCE GROUP	AMW	+50%	0.36 vs 0.24	+0%	+0.0%
HOLOGIC INC	HOLX	+50%	0.15 vs 0.10	+46%	+8.7%
WHITEHALL CORP	WHT	+45%↓	0.42 vs 0.29	+28%↓	+7.3%↑
APCO ARGENTINA INC CAY	APAGF	+44%↓	0.46 vs 0.32	+15%↓	+29.8%↑
RENTERS CHOICE INC	RCII	+36%↑	0.19 vs 0.14	+64%↓	+7.9%↑
MCGRATH RENTCORP	MGRC	+34%↓	0.59 vs 0.44	+34%↑	+17.5%↓
GARAN INCORPORATED	GAN	+32%↓	0.49 vs 0.37	+20%↑	+5.0%↓

Most Downs

COVENTRY CORP	CVTY	-80%↑	0.01 vs 0.05	+29%↑	+0.1%
CAMERON FINANCIAL CORP	CMRN	-77%	0.07 vs 0.30	+0%	+0.0%
MAPINFO CORP	MAPS	-71%↑	0.05 vs 0.17	-2%↓	+2.9%↑
SONICS & MATERIALS INC	SIMA	-60%↑	0.02 vs 0.05	+16%↓	+4.0%↑
BERLITZ INTL INC	BTZ	-55%↓	0.05 vs 0.11	+2%↑	+0.4%↑

Computer-Integrated Syst		Eps 32 Rel 73
Qtr. Sep 30:	1996 (AMEX)	1995
Sales -2%↑	3,254,000	3,332,000
Net Loss	-33,000	-177,000
Avg shares	8,996,000	6,190,000
Earn/shr	w....	-0.03
w – Nil.		

BATTERY TECHNOLOGIES INC		BTIOF 13/16
Consumer Products-Misc		Eps 49 Rel 7
Qtr. Sep 30:	1996 (OTC)	1995
Sales -84%↓	2,017,000	5,588,000

gain from the sale of property.

BRANDYWINE REALTY TRUST		BDN 5 15/16
Finance-Equity Reit		Eps 40 Rel 79
Qtr. Sep 30:	1996 (AMEX)	1995
Sales +191%↑	2,572,000	885,000
Net Loss	-129,000	-152,000
Avg shares	2,311,118	1,874,041
Earn/shr	-0.06	-0.08

| CAMBRIDGE SHOPPING CTR | | CBG.TO 9 9/32 |
| Real Estate Operations | | Eps 26 Rel 74 |

74 Downs
Median Change -35%

A P A OPTICS INC		APAT 5%
Elec-Laser Sys/Component		Eps 23 Rel 32
Qtr. Sep 30:	1996 (OTC)	1995
Sales -1%↑	672,666	682,828
Net Loss	-6,763	c14,795
Avg shares	8,160,736	7,623,839
Earn/shr	w....	w....
c – Income. w – Nil.		

ACCENT SOFTWARE INTL LTD		ACNTF 8 5/16
Computer-Software		Eps 1 Rel 2
Qtr. Sep 30:	1996 (OTC)	1995
Sales -53%↓	603,000	1,296,000
Net Loss	-5,726,000	-1,461,000
Avg shares	9,787,000	7,322,000
Earn/shr	-0.59	-0.20

ALKERMES INC		ALKS 14%
Medical-Biomed/Genetics		Eps 5 Rel 91
Qtr. Sep 30:	1996 (OTC)	1995
Sales +16%↑	4,082,188	3,529,711
Net Loss	-4,789,384	-2,960,194
Earn/shr	-0.26	-0.22

ALLEGRO NEW MEDIA INC		ANMI 5%
Computer-Software		Eps 15 Rel 27
Qtr. Sep 30:	1996 (OTC)	h1995
Sales +466%↑	1,687,889	298,342
Net Loss	k-6,629,322	-211,717
Avg shares	3,680,435	1,198,994
Earn/shr	-1.80	-0.25

h – Per share figures after preferred dividend requirements. k – Includes a charge of $3.89 mil related to Serif acquisition and a $2.14 mil charge for compensation expense.

ALTEON INC		ALTN 7%
Medical-Biomed/Genetics		Eps 11 Rel 14
Qtr. Sep 30:	1996 (OTC)	1995
Sales +36%↓	588,000	431,000
Net Loss	-5,346,000	-2,529,000
Avg shares	15,679,313	12,824,448
Earn/shr	-0.34	-0.20

ANCOR COMMUNICATIONS INC		ANCR 15%
Computer-Local Networks		Eps 11 Rel 95
Qtr. Sep 30:	1996 (OTC)	1995
Sales +42%↓	1,861,132	1,311,217
Net Loss	-1,192,920	-604,725
Avg shares	10,092,441	7,597,182
Earn/shr	-0.12	-0.08

| ARIELY ADVERTISING LTD | | RELEF 2% |
| Comml Svcs-Advertising | | Eps 7 Rel 4 |

EXHIBIT 6-1.   Corporate Earnings Reports.

from the prior quarter. In addition to the actual earnings and percentage gain, the company's after-tax profit margin is reported. An up or down arrow indicates whether a company's after-tax earnings have risen or declined over the prior quarter.

All companies that have announced their earnings are separated every day in alphabetical order into those whose earnings are up, and those whose earnings are down. At the beginning of the *Ups* section, the total number of firms that are reporting higher earnings, and their median change, is reported. Likewise, a total and median change are shown for the

Downs. This permits an overall feel of the market, since more companies will show rising earnings in an expanding economy, and more will have declining earnings during an economic slowdown.

Each concise company report on this page shows the closing price of its stock, its EPS rank, relative strength rank, industry group strength ranking, and stock symbol, plus the actual percentage change in earnings for the current quarter (Exhibit 6-1). Once again, an asterisk (*) is used to highlight those few companies whose current quarterly increases in earnings have exceeded 30 percent on a year-over-year basis *and* whose sales and earnings gains have both accelerated from the prior quarter. An up or down arrow indicates whether earnings and sales have accelerated or decelerated from the prior quarter. In some cases, quarterly earnings, sales, net income, and earnings over the last 6 to 9 months, compared with similar periods a year earlier, are also shown.

Companies with strong current earnings should have their earnings records of the previous quarters also examined to determine whether the latest figures are relatively stronger or weaker. Increases in the current quarter may be deceptively impressive if the year-earlier results for the same quarter were unusually depressed. Conversely, a strong latest report may have greater value if the same quarter a year earlier was also strong.

PRICE/EARNINGS RATIO

The *P/E ratio* of a stock is the market price of the stock divided by its company's earnings per share. The ratio expresses an elementary point—namely, that the price of a stock is a function of earnings, whether past, present, or future, and that the price of a stock is predicated upon its earning power. In fact, the P/E ratio was born out of a premise that price is driven by earnings.

When trailing (the past 4 quarters or past 12 months) earnings are used, the ratio is called a trailing P/E ratio, and this has been the conventional method for stock valuation. It is the trailing 12-month P/E that appears in most newspaper tables. It levels the playing field by covering the same period for all companies regardless of when their individual fiscal year ends. However, the actual values of the published trailing P/E ratios for the same company can show substantial variability between newsletters. This occurs because earnings as reported in income statements are subject to generally accepted accounting principles, and different databases interpret the same income statement differently to extract what they feel is the number that reflects true profits. This means that stocks should not be compared using P/E ratios from different published sources.

In simple terms, a P/E ratio tells the story of the ongoing relationship between the price of a stock and its earnings. This association can be clearly understood by plotting the long-term figures of stock prices and the annual earnings of a company together on the same graph. As the earnings gain or lose ground, the price line will oscillate around the earnings. The price line, relative to the earnings line, indicates whether a stock is cheap or expensive relative to earnings. A growth company becomes easily identified from such a chart because the earnings keep on a steady upward course, with earnings higher each year. A wide distance between the price and the earnings line at any time, with the price line above the earnings line, indicates that the price has been disproportionately bid up, and the stock is expensive. The best time to buy a stock is when the price line comes back to the earnings line or drops below it. When the two lines converge, it means the company's growth is equal to its P/E ratio, and this may be a good time to invest in future growth at a bargain price. When the price line is drifting away and upward from the earnings line, the company is no longer a bargain, despite good earnings.

The P/E ratio, therefore, measures what investors are willing to pay for each dollar of profits from a particular corporation at a particular time. The higher a stock's P/E ratio, the more one is paying to share in that company's profits. A stock selling at a P/E ratio of 20 means that its price is 20 times earnings. The ratio is considered to be a better standard to compare a company's value than the price of its stock. For example, a share of a company with a price of $20 but a P/E of 22.4 would be considered to be "cheaper" than a share of another company selling at $11 with a P/E of 56.1.

There are no absolute figures to quantify low or high P/Es, because there are different "normal" values for different corporations and industry groups. P/E ratios below 10 are an unusual occurrence, and those companies with P/Es below 5 usually either are in extreme financial difficulty, or are in an industry suffering from general neglect because of some bad news overhanging the industry group.[13] Higher P/Es, on the other hand, reflect a positive judgment by the market on the quality of the underlying company. High-growth companies typically have very high P/Es, because their stock prices can rise explosively when fueled by a perceived potential for very high future profits.

The P/E of a market index or market average is determined from the P/Es of its component stocks. It provides a valuation of the general market as a benchmark against which to measure the relative attractiveness of industry groups and individual stocks.

DIVIDEND YIELDS

Dividends represent a portion of earnings that are paid by a corporation in cash or as additional stock to its shareholders as a return on their investment. The law forbids the payment of dividends from capital, and limits their payment to be made only from earnings or retained earnings. Dividends, hence, are the result of earnings, and a record of dividend payments and increases in dividends has traditionally been a real measure of a company's financial history and of investor and management expectations. When expectations have been low, investors have required a higher dividend yield, and vice versa. A dividend rise or decline has also been conventionally viewed by the markets as a strong signal about management's expectations of a company's prospects, and a company's dividend announcement has always been an important and relevant item of information. Increases in dividends are always favorable. Dividend cuts have been associated with poor earnings performance, and have resulted in significant declines in stock prices.

The *dividend yield* of a stock or market average is obtained by dividing the current annualized dividend (the most recent quarterly dividend multiplied by 4) or the anticipated dividend (next 12 months) by the current price, and is expressed as a percentage. The figure can be calculated for a single stock, or for all the stocks in aggregate that form a market average or index. Common stocks have usually shown dividend yields ranging between 2.5 percent and 8 percent. Dividend yields are highest during periods of low stock prices, because dividend payments are less volatile than stock prices. When stock prices drop, corporations maintain dividends to sustain investor confidence, thus driving up the dividend yield. When yields are low, stock prices are high and generally overvalued, and low market yields have usually been followed by general declines in market prices. Low yields have also resulted from slow dividend growth. Conversely, high dividend yields may imply undervalued conditions with the prospect of rising prices.

When the dividend yield of the DJIA or the S&P 500 has been under 3 percent, there has been no instance of a rising market, and sizable market declines have frequently ensued.[14] At the other extreme, a dividend yield on the Dow exceeding 7 percent has invariably been followed by rising prices in the following 2 to 5 years (see discussion in Chapter 5).

BOOK VALUE

Book value is what a company is worth in dollars from an accounting point of view. It is the value, at the time of liquidation, of its assets minus the total of its liabilities and the par value of its preferred stock taken together. This dollar value can then be divided by the number of its outstanding common shares to determine book value per share. The figure gives an indication of what shareholders, as owners, would have left over for themselves after all assets have been sold or converted to cash, and all those with a prior claim have been satisfied.

Reliable book values cannot always be established, because the resale value of some assets such as plant and equipment could be minimal if they are old or obsolete, whereas other assets such as real estate could have appreciated substantially over time because of inflation. For the latter reason, book values can understate the replacement cost of underlying assets by significant amounts. This is also the reason that successful corporations are being sold almost constantly at prices well above their book value (net asset value): Fixed assets are usually recorded at historic cost (purchase price) minus the depreciation.

A stock does not become a sound investment merely because it can be purchased at close to its book value. Just because price is below book value does not mean that a stock is cheap. The reason may be that the value of its assets has been overstated, or there may be a past record, or future prospects, of poor earnings which may not be expected to improve sufficiently to justify a higher price. Good stocks will not sell below book value for long.

The price-to-book ratio of the Dow is determined by dividing its price by its prior year's book value. When the DJIA or the S&P 500 Index has sold at over 2 times book value, the market has been near or at a top; conversely, the DJIA has rarely traded at ratios substantially below 1.0.

HOW TO USE *INVESTOR'S BUSINESS DAILY* FOR FUNDAMENTAL ANALYSIS

THE NEW AMERICA: COMPUTERS AND TECHNOLOGY

Behind every successful market professional is a team of security research analysts whose task is to determine a company's intrinsic value after weighing all the known information about its economic, technical, and human resources and its competitive advantage. Every week, *Investor's Business Daily* provides individual investors with their own personal team of research analysts who present concise, in-depth reports on the ideas and people behind the leading companies in the leading industries. The stories behind these companies, their products and their management, their monopolies and their competition, form the basis of the unique *The New America* and the *Computers and Technology* sections found only in *Investor's Business Daily*. They supplement the proprietary quantitative information reported in the tables, charts, and data blocks to allow an individual investor to uncover stocks of companies that offer an unusually high expected return for their level of risk. Together, they provide the individual investor with the most powerful armamentarium assembled in a newspaper for fundamental security analysis.

The distinctive page on *The New America* is an invaluable source of information on the potential growth companies of the future. These are young and exciting corporations, alive with fresh ideas on new products, new technologies, and new ways of doing business. Every business day, three such fast-growing new companies are profiled, concisely yet in-depth. The bottom of this page forms a *New Issues* update that profiles, in a table, companies that plan to become public in the near future (*Recent IPO Filings*), and an update on the performance of those companies that have recently gone public (*Prices of Recent IPOs*). This is another page that should be saved and filed for future reference, for here is information on new ideas and on the growth stocks of tomorrow that is also not readily available elsewhere.

Leading *The New America* is an unprecedented wave of technological innovations. Like the Renaissance and the Industrial Revolution, the present era marks one of the great ages of humanity, characterized by a powerful social transformation. In our time, this marks the transition from an industrialized society to an electronic knowledge-based society, and an economic system based on knowledge. The factory worker is being replaced by the hi-tech intellectual. An expanded weekly section on *Computers and Technology* puts these evolving changes in proper investment perspective. It provides an understanding of the new ideas in technology, and interviews the people behind the new sciences to show how American corporations are preparing for the change, what they are doing to manage their existing information systems, and what new technology they are acquiring to prepare for the future. New trends in computers and technology are summarized here along with statistics, strategies, and analyses on the leading industries and companies that are piloting these changes, and which ones are worthy of more study for investment.

The Intelligent Tables

The two parameters that are most widely used to describe the intrinsic value of a corporation, or the overall market, are its P/E ratio and its dividend yield. Both parameters are reported every week for every company in the *Intelligent Tables*. The P/E ratio, dividend yield, and price-to-book ratio of the DJIA are shown daily in the box on *Psychological Market Indicators* in the *Market Charts* section (see Exhibit 5-1, Chapter 5). The additional information on Nasdaq stocks includes fundamental statistics on earnings (*% Annual Earnings Growth, % Qtr EPS, Annual Earnings Estimate*), sales (*% Qtr Sales*), P/E ratios (*P/E on Estimate*), and return on equity (*ROE*) (see Exhibit 2-3, Chapter 2). The ROE is calculated by dividing the average common stock equity in the past 2 years into the net income for the most recent year.

For purposes of investment, the return on equity (ROE) has been regarded as the single best measure of a firm's ability to generate a flow of income for dividends. ROE, sometimes called earnings power, indicates how well a company is being managed to allow a profit on its equity or net worth.[15] It is a measure of a company's rate of return on the money provided by its share owners, and is a useful indicator of what a company can earn in the future on the net income that it chooses to retain. The ROE, therefore, tells investors how effectively their money is being used. For growth companies, an ROE of 15 percent has been generally considered a minimum, and a current ROE below 15 percent should be viewed with concern. A favorable ROE is one that has been rising over time and is higher than the average ROE for all companies in a given industry.

A good business should be able to earn a good ROE without borrowing. The degree of a corporation's debt, or its financial leverage, will also influence ROE. Indeed, debt can allow an excellent ROE during good years, but can be detrimental when revenues have declined but interest costs on the debt have remained unchanged. The individual investor must make it a habit to look at the percentage debt (debt-to-equity ratio) and the ROE figures together to understand the validity of an ROE. Companies can raise their ROE significantly by increasing their percentage debt. For this reason, companies that are able to earn a good ROE only in good times by employing significant debt should be viewed with caution.

The number of a company's outstanding shares minus shares owned by management (*shares float*) is reported every day for every stock listed in the Nasdaq *Intelligent Tables*. This figure is also shown in each chart displayed in the *Stocks in the News* chart gallery and in *Your Weekend Graphic Review* section. A 38-year study of the greatest stock market winners concluded that 98 percent of these stocks had fewer than 25 million shares outstanding during the time of their winning performance. In another study, the average capitalization of the top market performers between 1970 to 1982 was 11.8 million shares, with a median value of 4.6 million *before* their big price moves.[16] A very large number of outstanding shares requires a greater volume of buying to raise the price because of the large supply of stock available. The more widely owned a stock and the larger its institutional following, the more likely that everything known about the stock is reflected in its price. On the other hand, market inefficiencies that lead to large profits are more likely to be realized with the smaller and less analyzed companies. Average returns on stocks with low market capitalization have been shown to be triple those of the largest companies.

COMPANIES IN THE NEWS

Additional information for the fundamental analysis of corporations is presented every day on those leading companies from leading industry groups that are currently showing strong market action. These data are displayed in a chart called *Industry Group Focus* on the *Companies in the News* page (see Exhibit 1-4, Chapter 1). The return on equity (ROE), debt-to-equity percentage (percentage debt), and net percentage profit margin (the "bottom line"), each calculated annually, are listed for each company. Total corporate debt should be below 35 percent of market capitalization for growth-stock companies; debt is particularly dangerous for cyclical companies. Long-term debt exceeding 50 percent of shareholder's equity is a risky condition. Sales and earnings over the last quarter and the 5-year high and low values for the P/E ratio are among the additional parameters identified here. Since these are the companies that are the most deserving of the investor's concentration, *Investor's Business Daily* can be used profitably every week for the fundamental analysis of over 100 leading corporations. The ROE and the percentage of equity that has been borrowed (percentage debt) are also shown in each chart displayed in the *Stocks in the News* gallery (Exhibit 7-3, Chapter 7), and in *Your Weekend Graphic Review* section. Hence, the ROE and corporate debt (percentage debt) of several hundred leading corporations can be tracked every week in *Investor's Business Daily.*

The most intensive coverage on a single company that can be available in any financial newspaper is displayed in the *Companies in the News* section. Every day, an industry group that has ranked in the top 25 percent in performance over the prior 6 months is selected, and companies in this industry that have demonstrated the strongest earnings and price performances are chosen for review. The page displays three graphs that together reveal the short-, intermediate-, and long-term financial picture. The top large graph reports up to 150 basic analytical items on the company. Below that is a proprietary *Daily Graph* that charts daily price and volume history for the past 12 months, along with additional fundamental and technical information. The final smaller graph is a long-term chart covering monthly prices and volume going back 15 years.

It has been true of the investment experience that the years teach much that the days never knew. Long-term charts offer the clearest picture of cyclical price trends. By looking backward, long-term charts provide a fresh perspective on where a stock is now and how it got there. They present a view of the size of the price base, the major price trend, its historical support and breakout levels, and the stock's upside potential, whereas the daily graph allows the determination of the precise time and price level for actual buying. The daily graph picks up approximately where the long-term graph leaves off, and the daily chart becomes more useful once the weekly picture has become significant.

NOTES

1. The classic reference on fundamental analysis is the book by Benjamin Graham currently in its fifth edition: Sidney Cottle, Roger Murray, and Frank Block, *Graham & Dodd's Security Analysis* (McGraw-Hill, NY, 1988). Additional good sources are Benjamin Graham's *The Intelligent Investor* (Harper & Row, NY, 1973), Al Frank's *The Prudent Speculator* (Dow Jones Irwin, Homewood, IL, 1990), Stanley Huang's *Techniques of Investment Analysis* (Intext, Scranton, PA, 1972), Norman Fosback, *Stock Market Logic* (Dearborn Financial Publishing, 1991), Charles Brandes' *Value Investing Today* (Dow Jones Irwin, Homewood, IL, 1989), Lawrence Stein's *Value Investing* (John Wiley & Sons, NY, 1987), and Martin Whitman and Martin Schubik's *The Aggressive Conservative Investor* (Random House, NY, 1979). Stein's book is the best single book for the individual investor, and should be part of one's personal library.

2. Frank, *Prudent Speculator*. See also Robert Hagstrom Jr., *The Warren Buffett Way* (John Wiley & Sons, NY, 1994).

3. William J. O' Neil, *How to Make Money in Stocks* (McGraw-Hill, NY, 1991).

4. *Ibid.*

5. *Ibid.*

6. This paragraph has been put together from Frank, *Prudent Speculator*; Diana Harrington, Frank Fabozzi, and H. Russell Fogler, *The New Stock Market* (Probus Publishing, Chicago, 1990); and Geraldine Weiss and Janet Lowe, *Dividends Don't Lie* (Dearborn Financial Publishing Inc., 1989).

7. Harrington, Fabozzi, and Fogler, *New Stock Market*.

8. *Ibid.*

9. William O'Neil, *How to Make Money in Stocks* (McGraw-Hill, NY, 1991).

10. *Ibid.*

11. *Ibid.*

12. Investor's Business Daily, *Guide to High-Performance Investing* (O'Neil Data Systems Inc., Los Angeles, 1993).

13. Martin Zweig, *Winning on Wall Street* (Warner Books, NY, 1990).

14. Stein, *Value Investing.*

15. A good discussion on ROE can be found in Gerald Perrit, *Small Stocks, Big Profits* (Dearborn Financial Publishing, 1993), from which the following discussion has been put together. Strategies that can be used to increase ROE are outlined in Alfred Rapaport, *Creating Shareholder Value* (The Free Press, NY, 1986). See also Hagstrom, *The Warren Buffett Way.*

16. William O'Neil, *How to Make Money in Stocks.*

THE INTERNAL STRUCTURE OF MARKETS[1]

Technical analysis represents an objective system for determining the appropriate time to buy or sell a stock only on the basis of market data and not the business records or prospects of the companies themselves. It relies upon the past behavior of stock prices to determine with some exactitude the direction of the future. This involves weighing the evidence to determine the probability that the ingredients of a bull market are at hand. If the elements are there, and the level of confidence in them is high, then portfolio allocations can be adjusted to profit from the bull market.

Observations on the movements of stock prices have led to the development of a multitude of indicators and graphic chart patterns whose value, when correct, has been to improve the timing of asset allocation or asset conversion—that is, the appropriate time to move from securities to cash or from cash to securities. Understanding the logic behind technical indicators, what makes them work and why their message may change, has often required analyses of decades of historical data. Despite an impressive legacy in technical analysis, a perfect market timing indicator has never been found. Hindsight has revealed some virtually perfect examples, but they have often betrayed their followers in real time. The lessons of history have also shown that the best indicators are simple and operate on general information that is widely available; the stock market is not susceptible to esoteric, highly mathematical formulations, or even to scientific insight.

Market timing can return substantial profits to the individual investor who has made a thorough economic and fundamental analysis. More commonly, market-timing techniques have indicated what not to do rather than what to do. They have forced trades to occur in gear with the major market trend, thus allowing purchases to be acquired on strength, and sales to be made during periods of market weakness.

There has been no accepted explanation proposed for the rationale of technical analysis, but it probably has its roots in the psychology of buying and selling. Stock markets are an auction process where buyers and sellers come together to agree upon a price. When investors see a particular stock rise, they buy into the rise, so that each price rise helps fuel more enthusiasm in a self-fulfilling prophecy, thus creating an uptrend. A market trend, therefore, feeds upon itself. The longer the market keeps going up and, consequently, the nearer it must be to its top, the more speculators enter on the scene and buy shares, attracted by the great activity and the stories of huge gains. Therefore, if buying continues and supply is being absorbed, the market will continue to advance.[2] If buying is weak, then the selling will overwhelm the bid and push the market down. Chart patterns are a visual representation of this auction process.

HOW TO USE *INVESTOR'S BUSINESS DAILY* TO DRAW TRENDLINES

An important step in chart analysis is to identify when a change of trend is likely to occur or whether it has already occurred. This can be done by drawing accurate *trendlines* on the three large market charts that are presented on the *Market Charts* page. Note that the three charts are drawn to the same horizontal time scale, so that confirmations of trends and their reversals for the three main unmanaged market indexes can be followed directly. Uptrend lines are drawn by connecting the lower points of a stock market's movement. A downtrend line must be drawn by connecting the higher points. This is an important distinction; the uninstructed have quite naturally done the opposite—namely, drawn uptrends from the upper limits, and downtrends from the lower ones.[3]

The uptrend line must be drawn upward, from the lowest low at the start of the time period under consideration to the highest low point preceding the highest high (Exhibit 7-1). The line must not pass through any other price values between these two points; that is, all prices between the two points must lie above the trendline.[4] This is another important distinction: Not only the closing prices but the full trading range of prices every day must be above the uptrend line. The trendline is now extended past the highest high point.[5] The slope of this line would be a close approximation of the slope obtained by performing a statistical linear regression analysis on the price data over the same time period. Once an uptrend has been established, subsequent declines toward the trend-line can be used as buying opportunities.

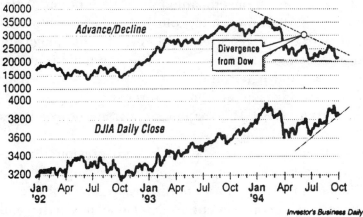

Crossing Trends

As the Dow moved higher, the A/D line failed to confirm the advance.

EXHIBIT 7-1.   The NYSE A-D Line and the DJIA.

Likewise, for a downtrend within a predetermined time period, a line is drawn from the highest high point to the lowest high point preceding the lowest low. Once again, the line must not pass through any other price values between these two points; that is, all intervening prices must lie below the downtrend line.[6] The trendline is now extended downward past the lowest high point.

The art of identifying an authentic trend is not a simple one to master. It is easy to see a trend *after* it has become well established, and trends stand out clearly on charts of past market action. The harder task is to identify a trend early in its evolution. Because trendlines are more easily recognized after they form, it may be necessary to start with a family of tentative trendlines. If there seem to be conflicting trends, draw them all as separate trendlines until one is corroborated by the newer points.[7] Often a trendline that looks correct may have to be redrawn. When a price penetrates through a trend line, allow the original line to remain and draw in a new alternate; when the authentic line has been verified, the erroneous one can be erased.[8]

HOW TO USE TRENDLINES

Trendlines have been used to generate buy or sell signals, because there has rarely been an important change in a price trend that has not been accompanied by a penetration of the trendline on a chart. However, trendlines have been notorious for being penetrated prematurely, and considerable judgment is needed in deciding where to place a trendline and in determining when a valid penetration has occurred.[9] The proper placing of a trendline is an art that matures with one's remembrances of markets past: The shape and position of trendlines are largely a matter of judgment.

New stock purchases may be made, and previous investments should be held, as long as an established uptrend line remains intact. Any break in a trendline, especially if it occurs on higher volume, becomes a cue to defer new purchases and reexamine existing stock holdings. If a stock drops more than 3 percent below its uptrend line, or more than 5 percent in a strong bull market, it is time to liquidate.[10] Alternatively, if a stock reverses after a steady rise and declines below the previous trough, then confirmatory evidence of an actual trend reversal is given. Evidence of a downtrend indicates that it is time to sell or take other defensive measures to avoid losses. Even the most perfect trendlines suffer the handicap of all trend-following investment strategies: Signs of trend reversal appear well after a peak or trough in prices, and a large part of a total price move can be lost.

Changes in volume are important, and often have warned of reversals in trends before their actual occurrence. If a series of ascending peaks in an uptrend is accompanied by successively lower volume, the advance is weakening as volume is no longer going with the trend. Climactic price actions, and their associated heavy volumes, have also heralded reversals in market prices.

HOW TO USE *INVESTOR'S BUSINESS DAILY* FOR TIMING THE MARKET WITH MOVING AVERAGES

The technique of using moving averages for profit—that is, to generate a "buy" or a "sell" signal—has involved the simultaneous use of a moving-average line and its stock or market index prices. For this reason, moving averages are shown on the same chart as the market index or stock prices. Look at the moving-average line in the chart in Exhibit 7-2. (See also the discussion in Chapter 1.) The chart shows the closing prices of the Dow Jones Industrials from the end of June 1994 to the end of March 1995. The 200-day moving average is represented by the dotted line. The DJIA in June is below its moving-average line and rising. It oscillates around the moving-average line until the end of August, when it penetrates the line upward from below. Thereafter, it remains predominantly just above the moving-average line until mid-November, when it penetrates the moving-average line once again, but this time from above to below. It now stays predominantly below its moving average for about 4 weeks. In mid-

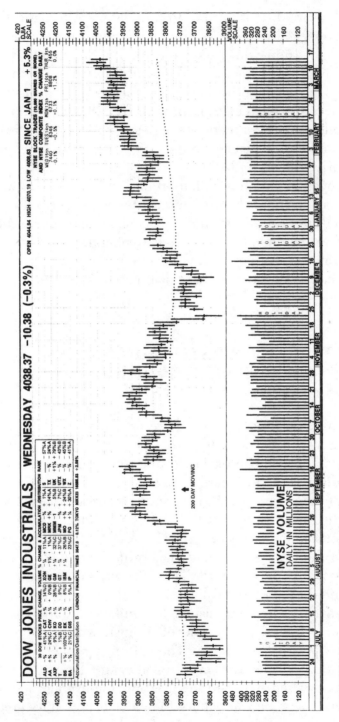

EXHIBIT 7-2. How to Use Moving Averages.

December, it penetrates the moving-average line from below on high volume. There is a pullback of prices to the moving-average line, a correction, and then the DJIA takes off to reach a new high at 4034 on high volume.

Now look at the trend of the moving-average line itself. It is sloping upward in June 1994, but the slope flattens out and moves downward slightly toward the end of the year. Stocks may be purchased in mid-August, because the DJIA has penetrated upward above the moving-average line and the moving-average line itself is still moving upward. However, conditions are certainly adverse for stocks in mid-November. Not only has the DJIA penetrated the moving-average line on the downside, but the moving-average line itself has flattened out and turned downward. This is a sell signal. By early 1995, however, the trend has again changed and the moving average has flattened out and turned upward once more. A strong buy signal is clearly in place in early February 1995. Not only has the DJIA penetrated its moving average on the upside in late December, but the moving-average line itself has now turned upward. This would be the time to buy.

In summary, the two fundamental rules to determine buy or sell signals from the moving averages shown on the Market Charts page are:[11]

1. A buy signal is generated when the 200-day moving-average line flattens out after a previous decline and turns upward and, at the same time, prices penetrate the moving-average line on the upside.

2. A sell signal is generated when the 200-day moving-average line flattens out following a previous rise and starts declining and, simultaneously, prices penetrate the moving-average line on the downside.

During the initial stages of a bull market, both the Dow and its moving average move up together. The first market correction, which could represent an intermediate trend, may send the Dow price down to bounce off the moving-average line or even penetrate it downward. This may not necessarily be a sell signal; rarely, if a market correction is severe, the moving-average line may turn down as well. The Dow and its moving average will normally turn back up and go on to new highs. This second upturn should be followed more closely, since downturns after this stage may indicate true market deterioration and a sell signal.[12] During the initial stages of a bear market, both the Dow and its moving average move down together.

Much has been written about the message of moving averages. For example, prices are said to be trending up when a 3-day simple moving average crosses above a 12-day moving average, and prices are trending down when the 3-day moving average drops below the 12-day moving average.[13] A trading range has been defined by a 4-day moving average having a value between the 9-day and 12-day moving averages; a trending market occurs when all three are moving in the same direction.[14] The slope of a single moving-average line can also be useful; the greater the rate of change or the steeper its slope, the stronger a trend. A horizontal or near-horizontal moving-average line indicates a flat market in a narrow trading range.[15] If a 13-day exponential moving average has not reached a new high or low in one month, this also indicates that the market is in a trading range.[16]

The sensitivity of a moving average and the reliability of its signals depend on the volatility of the price of the index or security being tracked, and the time frame used to calculate the moving average.[17] The advantage of any form of averaging has been that it allows a smoothing of the data, with the degree of smoothing being determined by the length (time period) of the average: Longer moving averages have shown better smoothing than their shorter counterparts. But to this must be added the drawback of delay. The longer the period encompassed by a moving average, the less current is its graph. When subject to smoothing (averaging), indicator peaks have their major turning points preserved, but lagging the unsmoothed raw data that they seek to represent. By the time a long-term moving average turns, the price itself will usually be well on its way in the new direction. Hence, moving averages are always out of date. A 2-week average is 1 week out of date, whereas a 52-week average is lagging by many weeks.

HOW TO USE *INVESTOR'S BUSINESS DAILY* FOR TIMING INDIVIDUAL STOCKS WITH MOVING AVERAGES

The same rules that apply to the market averages have been extended to individual stocks. Stocks should not be purchased when prices are below their moving averages, and selling stocks should be avoided as long as prices remain above their moving-average line.[18] Ten-week simple moving-average lines are shown every day in the chart gallery of individual stocks that make up the *Stocks in the News* (Exhibit 7-3), and every Friday in the similar stock charts that are presented in *Your Weekend Graphic Review*. The display of moving-average lines on individual stock charts is unique to *Investor's Business Daily,* and cannot be found in any other newspaper.

Some investors track 10-week and 30-week moving averages to span both a short- and a long-range perspective. The longer-term moving average moves more deliberately, and its crossover by the shorter average line, bullish on the upside or bearish to the downside, is viewed as an important indicator of a trend change. The general idea is that a price penetration of the short-term moving average signals a reversal of the minor trend, whereas a price penetration of both moving averages signals a major reversal of trend. If the current price of a stock is higher than the 10-week moving average which, in turn, is higher than the 30-week moving average, then a favorable situation is in place. Positions should be taken only in the direction of the long-term trend as determined by the latest penetration of the longer-term moving average. The shorter-term average serves better for liquidating positions and for reinstating them in the direction of the major trend.[19] Moving averages, thus, allow risks to be automatically limited and losses to be minimized; likewise, positions can be automatically estab-

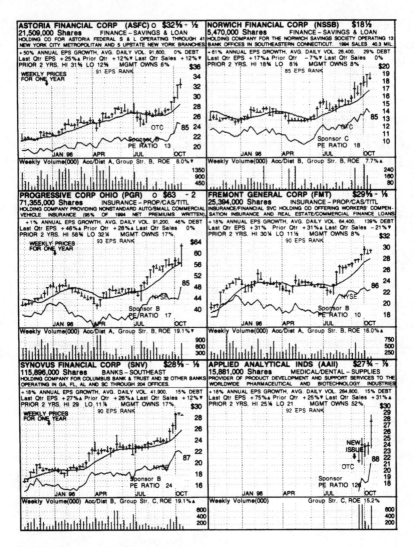

EXHIBIT 7-3. Stocks in the News.

lished in the right direction at the onset of a sustained move, and this tends to maximize profits.

Such a pair of moving-average lines is displayed every day in *Investor's Business Daily* on the large stock chart on the *Companies in the News* page. A 10-week moving-average line and a 200-day moving-average line are drawn.

PERCENTAGE OF NYSE STOCKS ABOVE THEIR 200-DAY MOVING AVERAGES[20]

The percentage of NYSE stocks trading above their 200-day moving averages is shown on the *Market Charts* page in *Investor's Business Daily* (see Exhibit 1-5, Chapter 1). It is located in the top left corner of the large chart of the Dow Jones Industrials on this page.

One way of applying moving averages to evaluate the breadth of the market has been to determine the number of stocks in a broad market, such as the NYSE, which are in a positive trend. *Investor's Business Daily* is the only newspaper that does this every day by calculating the 200-day moving averages of all NYSE stocks, and then determining the percentage of that number whose prices are above their moving averages. This figure serves as a coincident indicator of the breadth of the market. When this percentage is above 50 percent, the outlook has been bullish; when below 50 percent, the forecast is bearish. The indicator has shown a 66 percent reliability of predicting the market trend over the following year. It has often proved beneficial to convert this reported daily value itself into a simple 5-week moving average, and then plot it with the DJIA to accentuate the divergences.

The market is undergoing internal deterioration when the DJIA holds but the percentage of stocks on the NYSE that are over their moving averages declines. When this percentage is at a low level and moving up, it is time to be invested in the market. When the indicator is at a high level and moving down, it is time to become defensive and move out of the market. It has been proposed that values over 80 percent represent an overbought market which is due for a decline (upward momentum fades), and values below 20 percent reflect an oversold market that could be ready for an advance (the market is unreasonably low). Values below 60 percent generally indicate imminent declining market trends. Extreme values (10 to 15 percent or 90 to 100 percent) point out that a major market move has already occurred but not necessarily that it has reached an end. Changes in direction from such an extreme would be a sign that the primary market direction is about to reverse.

It has been suggested that a stronger market trading signal is generated when the percentage of NYSE stocks that are over their moving averages is combined with the sentiment indicator of investment advisory firms that is put together by *Investor's Intelligence*. This sentiment indicator is also shown on the same *Market Charts* page in the box of *Psychological Market Indicators*. A strong bullish signal is given when the percentage of NYSE stocks moving-average indicator is moving up from below 30 percent, and the sentiment indicator shows lots of bearish advisers, as was the case in October 1990. A strong bearish signal is given when the moving-average indicator is moving down from above 70 percent with lots of bullish advisers, as was seen in September 1987.

SUPPORT AND RESISTANCE LEVELS[21]

In simple terms, a stock can move up (uptrend), down (downtrend), or sideways (consolidation). Clues to turning points in stock price trends have been provided by support and resistance levels. Investors who are holding a fallen stock and are anxious to sell out their shares from a fear of further declines do so at the first opportunity that would allow them to break even. This occurs when fallen prices have risen back to levels at which the stocks were initially bought, and it is this price level that forms the "resistance" levels on the charts. Selling at the resistance levels causes rising prices to stop rising and move sideways, until a new round of enthusiasm can cause renewed buying, leading to a price breakout.

On the other hand, the chart price pattern described as a "support" area causes falling prices to stop falling and move sideways, or even reverse direction to break out on the upside. Good support indicates the willingness of sufficient buyers to absorb any and all shares offered for sale, even to the extent of overwhelming the sellers and creating a price breakout. Support levels have usually involved a 35 percent to 65 percent retracement of the major trend.

HOW TO USE *INVESTOR'S BUSINESS DAILY* TO MONITOR THE NYSE A-D LINE

An advance-decline (A-D) line is the difference between the *number* of stocks that advance in price and the *number* that decline on the NYSE (see Chapter 1). The daily NYSE A-D line is displayed every day in *Investor's Business Daily* on the *Market Charts* page. It is drawn below the price action of the S&P 500. Since the large chart of the Dow Jones Industrials is also shown with the same horizontal time scale, the price trend of the Dow and S&P 500, the 200-day moving-average line of the Dow and S&P 500, and the NYSE A-D line can all be examined simultaneously to look for divergences.

The market has been deemed bullish when the advance-decline line is moving upward, or it is performing better than the DJIA (Exhibit 1-5). On the other hand, when the DJIA reaches a peak that is not confirmed by a new high level in the advance-decline line, a market reversal of at least secondary proportions can be expected.[22] If the Dow continues to make a few more consecutive daily highs, and the advance-decline line keeps declining, a primary bear trend is likely to follow. In February 1994, for example, the NYSE A-D line peaked when the Dow was near an all-time high of 3975 (Exhibit 7-1). However, when the Dow rallied again in September to 3953, the A-D line was unable to confirm this strength. In fact, the trend of the A-D line was distinctly downward when the Dow was in an uptrend. This indicated that underneath the strong façade of the 30 Dow stocks, the broad market as represented by the NYSE was actually eroding substantially. The NYSE A-D line was lagging on the upside and leading on the downside, underscoring the rising risk in the market.

Many bull market peaks have been predicted by the advance-decline line. However, in any comparison between the advance-decline line and the DJIA, it is important to appreciate that there has always been an inherent long-term downward bias in the daily A-D line, thus making uptrends more difficult to realize. This downward bias has produced more occasions of negative divergences wherein the daily A-D line has moved lower and the DJIA has trended upward. As a result, the A-D line has been imprecise during market uptrends when the A-D line may sometimes veer downward much before the actual top in a bull market.[23]

The A-D line indicates the probability of a trend reversal, but it does not say when this event will take place. Divergences between the Dow and the A-D line preceded the market tops by months in 1959, 1961, 1972, and 1981. The rallies to a multiple top in 1937, 1946, and 1957 were also preceded by a divergence on the part of the A-D line.[24] In 1987, the A-D line began to diverge from the Dow in March. It was a valid signal for the October crash, but the poor breadth performance continued through the 500-point summer rally. Hence, it was a premature signal, because acting on the signal when it first occurred would have precluded any profits from the summer rally.

The A-D line has not been a particularly effective indicator of primary bottoms. The advance-decline line and the DJIA have reached their low points together about 70 percent of the time and, in some instances, the Dow has even been the earlier to bottom out. It has therefore been preferable to use the Dow signals, instead of the NYSE A-D line, at primary bear market bottoms for new buying opportunities. On some occasions, the A-D line has had some use in validating bear market rallies by its divergences.[25]

HOW TO USE *INVESTOR'S BUSINESS DAILY* TO MONITOR VOLUME OF TRADING

Every price change in a stock occurs as a result of a transaction consisting of either a purchase or a sale of the shares of the stock. The number of shares involved in such a transaction constitutes its volume. It is measured in hundreds of shares, or "round lots," unless otherwise indicated. The daily trading volume on the NYSE is displayed every day in *Investor's Business Daily* at the bottom of the chart of the DJIA on the *Market Charts* page. It is recorded as a vertical bar extending up from zero to the correct figure, in accordance with a scale along the side (Exhibit 7-2).

Volume is a measure of the direction of the market pressure for buying or selling. It reflects the intensity or conviction behind a move in prices, and has been regarded as a test of market strength or weakness. It has been known since the turn of the century that volume dominates and alters prices, tending to precede and predict their future trend. It is a relative measurement, since what is high volume in one phase of a market cycle may be considered light in another phase. In general, absolute daily volume over 200 million shares has been considered heavy, and that below 100 million shares is regarded as being thin.

High volume confirms price trends. Price and volume have generally moved in the same direction during the continuation of a prevailing trend. Put another way, volume should increase or expand in the direction of the existing price trend, and the higher the volume, the greater the significance of a price movement. In an uptrend, volume should be heavier as the price moves higher, and should decrease or contract on price declines.[26] Diminishing volume as prices advance indicates that demand is drying up at the higher price levels, and the market is becoming unfavorable. This is the usual situation during a selling climax. Subsequent rallies, however, must occur on expanding volume, even though the absolute volume may well be below that seen during the selling climax.

Changes in volume reflect a shift in crowd psychology associated with a particular price level, and have commonly heralded reversals in the trend of a market price movement before their actual occurrence. High volume associated with declining prices represents a divergence, and indicates a weak market resulting from an excessive or mounting supply of stock at the lower price levels. If prices and volume both decline, the lack of selling pressure signifies an improving situation, and prices should start rising again. This association in a bear market is a bullish sign, and the situation becomes especially optimistic if price subsequently breaks out on the upside on high volume. Very low volume really means an absence of buyers, since sellers are always present. When demand is lacking, this omnipresent selling pressure is the force that drives prices lower.

HOW TO USE *INVESTOR'S BUSINESS DAILY* TO DETECT CHART PATTERNS

Stocks can trace a potentially unlimited number of chart patterns. Pattern recognition models are based on the premise that chart movements of prices often play themselves out in predictable ways. For proper interpretation, price patterns must be confirmed by appropriate volume changes. Signals generated by chart patterns of individual stocks should be understood in the context of the general market activity, the activity of the industry group to which the stock belongs, and the relationship between the current stock price and its historic price scale.

Pattern recognition relies significantly on the perception that a given analyst has for a given chart. Reputable chartists have known for long that it is not easy to decide upon a course of action when a particular signal is generated, and the subjective nature of chart interpretation has become apparent from the not uncommon experience that renowned market professionals have come to different conclusions, and have given different recommendations, from the same universe of chart information. It is commonplace that technical analysts will agree on the figures but will dispute upon their meaning. A downturn signaled by a chart pattern when the general market and industry group are declining clearly constitutes a strong sell signal. More often, however, chart patterns generate signals when the market may offer no decisive clues, and activity in an industry group may remain, at best, mixed.

One of the consistently profitable chart patterns is the *cup-with-handle* configuration.[27] In this pattern, a chart of the closing prices of a stock over a period of 3 to 6 months (range: 7 to 65 weeks) looks like the outline of a cup when viewed from the side (Exhibit 7-4). The bottom of the cup's profile should be rounded and give the appearance of a U rather than a V.

A cup-with-handle pattern arises when a growth stock's price is declining during a natural correction.[28] Typically, such patterns are more commonly seen during the early stages of a bull market and during intermediate-term corrections. The

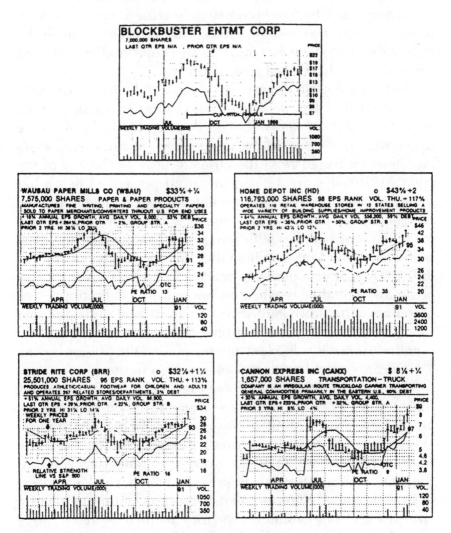

EXHIBIT 7-4.   The Cup-with-Handle Chart Pattern.

stock should have risen at least 30 percent before a cup-with-handle correction pattern appears, and in many instances a stock may have already doubled or tripled in price. Hence, such a stock is usually a fundamentally sound one and has experienced much accumulation. The left side of the cup's profile represents the downtrend that is correcting the previous uptrend. The stock's price then forms a broad bottom represented by the cup's rounded bottom. The bottom of the cup is accompanied by low volume, indicating a lack of selling pressure. From this bottom, prices will rise again, forming the right side of the cup to complete the cup's profile and then level off as the handle is being outlined.

The most important part of the cup's profile is its right side and the handle. The right side should form on rising volume, which is a sign of demand. The handle should form in the upper half, preferably in the upper third, of the overall cup's profile as measured from the absolute peak to the low of the cup.[29] Most cups are 12 percent to 20 percent in depth but some may be as much as 40 percent. Moreover, the level of the handle should be above the stock's 200-day moving-average price line. The handle itself evolves over 1 to 2 weeks and must have a downward price drift so that the price at the end of this drift is lower than a price low made a few weeks earlier.[30] This price low should be reached on low volume, indicating a lack of sellers. The downward drift of the handle indicates that there is still much pessimism in the stock at this point, and therefore there is sufficient money potentially present in the sidelines to launch the stock into new high territory.

The handle sets the stage for the stock's breakout to new highs. Stock prices can take off dramatically on high volume after the completion of a cup-and-handle price structure. When the stock breaks out from its handle, volume must rise by 40 percent above its 50-day average volume, thus confirming that enough demand is present at the stock's earliest emerging point.[31] Such stocks usually show improving relative strength and high volume just prior to their meteoric price takeoff, and can be detected by **boldfacing** in the *Intelligent Tables* and by their appearances in the data block showing the *greatest percentage rise in volume*.

Poorly formed cup-with-handle configurations typically show very deep or short cups whose bottoms look like a V instead of a U, or have handles forming too early in the lower third of the cup's profile and/or forming below the stock's 200-day moving average. Handles that have an updrift are unreliable. Such profiles result in failure. Cup depths of more than 45 percent are too excessive, because they make it difficult for the stock to break out successfully when the pattern is completed. Failure-prone patterns are also more likely to arise toward the end of a bull market cycle.

HOW TO USE *INVESTOR'S BUSINESS DAILY* FOR TECHNICAL ANALYSIS

A singular distinction in technical analysis, as opposed to fundamental analysis, is the recognition that the investor is never buying or selling a company but is bidding and offering in an auction.[32] There is no higher order that dictates the fate of market prices—just the human-made forces of purchases and sales, of support and resistance, that decide what has happened and what is happening. The battle for investment survival and stock market profits is fought on the playing fields of the market charts, and from these arise the variety of technical indicators that measure how the tide of battle has shifted. They promise neither perfection nor prophecy, but together they open an unemotional window into the reality of the internal market structure that churns beneath the neat façade of market prices. And after they have spoken, there still remains the burden of sifting the evidence, weighing the probabilities, and then making a decision and acting on it.[33]

A TECHNICAL ANALYSIS TOOL KIT

There is no limit to the variety of data that can be subject to technical analysis, and there is no good purpose in tracking too many indicators. One necessary set of information has always been the price action of the investment itself. Two trend-following indicators to identify divergences, a couple of timing guides to identify turning points, and a few to track the sentiments of those that move the markets will raise enough questions to allow the investor to decide whether the market is all that it is supposed to be. To this end, the moving-average and the advance-decline lines have withstood the test of decades in detecting the trends of stock or market indexes and, coupled with the common unmanaged market averages, have exposed divergences when many have been beguiled by the Dow's apparent health. The same may be said regarding divergences between the DJIA and the percentage of NYSE stocks that are above their 200-day moving averages. Divergence analysis is a powerful tool in technical analysis; when properly used, its message has carried a confidence reaching 99.5 percent that it is not due to chance alone.[34] The number of new highs or new lows has its roots in quintessential stock market behavior, and a simple 10-day advance/decline ratio has remained the oldest among the overbought/oversold oscillators.

Investor's Business Daily provides the individual investor with this complete arsenal. Most of it is already plotted on its daily charts and tables for the technical analysis of the stock market in general, and the most active individual stocks in particular.

A GALLERY OF CHARTS

The foundation of technical analysis lies in the study of charts and graphs, and *Investor's Business Daily* presents, on average, several hundred charts of individual stocks over the course of each week. Such an unprecedented wealth of chart patterns on the strongest and best-performing stocks cannot be found in any other daily newspaper. These charts allow the investor to draw trendlines, mark levels of resistance and support, identify important chart patterns, and determine key reversal patterns on the actively traded or top-performing stocks that are making the news.

Virtually every graph of stock prices in *Investor's Business Daily* has its own moving-average line. In the daily *Stocks in the News* sections and *Your Weekend Graphic Review*, published every Friday, a 10-week moving average is used (Exhibit 7-3). The more comprehensive analysis of a company in the *Companies in the News* section shows both 50-day and 200-day moving averages, since it is often better to use two moving averages: one giving a short-term trend and the other a longer-term one. Closing values of the stock market indexes (S&P 500 Index and the Dow Jones Industrials) are shown graphically with their own 200-day moving averages on the *Market Charts* page (see Exhibits 1-5 and 1-6, Chapter 1).

A daily A-D line of all the stocks on the New York Stock Exchange (NYSE) is plotted on the *Market Charts* page in the chart showing the S&P 500 (see Exhibit 1-5, Chapter 1). The exact number of stocks that have advanced or declined in price, and the number of stocks whose prices have remained unchanged over the previous day's trading, are listed just below the daily A-D line. From these values, a variety of the A/D ratios that have been described can be constructed (see reference 1). The absolute volume (total number of shares) of advancing and declining stocks, and that of unchanged issues, is also shown (see Exhibit 1-6, Chapter 1). A weekly A-D line of the NYSE is displayed on the same page in the chart showing the Dow Jones Industrials (see Exhibit 1-5, Chapter 1).

New highs and new lows can be found on the page indicated in the Contents as *New Highs and Lows* (see Exhibit 2-2, Chapter 2). From these values, a variety of high-low indicators that have been described can be constructed (see reference 1).

NOTES

1. There are many books on technical analysis, market timing, and specific technical indicators. Most general books on investment invariably carry a chapter or section on technical analysis. The generally accepted, though relatively expensive, reference books are Robert Colby and Thomas Meyers, *The Encyclopedia of Technical Market Indicators* (Dow Jones Irwin, Homewood, IL, 1988); Martin Pring, *Technical Analysis Explained* (McGraw-

Hill, NY, 1991); and Robert Edwards and John Magee, *Technical Analysis of Stock Market Trends* (John Magee Inc., Boston, 1992). John Murphy's *Technical Analysis of the Futures Markets* (NYIF, NY, 1986), though directed to futures, may well be the best reference book even for the regular stock market because of the clarity of its expression and the comprehensiveness of its coverage. The volume by Alexander Elder, *Trading for a Living* (John Wiley & Sons, NY, 1993), is also a recommended compendium of technical analysis with excellent practical examples and rules.

An outstanding companion for the individual investor is the trilogy by Justin Mamis: *How to Buy* (Farrar, Straus, Giroux, NY, 1982), *When to Sell*, with Robert Mamis (Simon & Schuster, NY, 1977), and *The Nature of Risk* (Addison-Wesley, NY, 1992). These very readable pocket-size editions get under the skin of technical analysis, unfolding the look and feel of the technical systems with real-life examples. Every effort should be made by individual investors to acquire this set. The value of its lessons continues to unfold after repetitive reading and study. Equal praise is merited by the writings of Gerald Appel, especially his *Winning Stock Market Systems* (Signalert Corp, Great Neck, NY, 1974), and, more recently, the works of Victor Sperandeo embodied in his two volumes *Trader Vic: Methods of a Wall Street Master* (John Wiley & Sons, NY, 1992) and *Trader Vic II: Principles of Professional Speculation* (John Wiley & Sons, NY, 1994).

An invaluable and instructive reference source, and just a pure delight to read, that explores the traditional as well as the uncharted realms of the technical analysis universe are the bound volumes (Vol.1 starts from 1982/83) and the current issues of the magazine *Technical Analysis of Stocks and Commodities* (3517 S.W. Alaska Street, PO Box 46518, Seattle, WA 98146-0518).

Books on investment systems based on technical analysis that also serve as very good introductions to the nature of technical analysis for the individual investor are Martin Zweig's *Winning on Wall Street* (Warner Books, NY, 1990), Stan Weinstein's *Secrets of Profiting in Bull and Bear Markets* (Dow Jones Irwin, IL, 1988), and Norman Fosback's *Stock Market Logic* (Dearborn Financial Publishing, 1976). They are available as paperbacks and merit study.

2. Thom Hartle, "Elementary Bond Trends," *Technical Analysis of Stocks and Commodities,* Vol. 8, 1990, p. 304.

3. William Jiler, *How Charts Can Help You in the Stock Market* (Trendlines, NY, 1962).

4. Sperandeo, *Trader Vic.*

5. *Ibid.*

6. *Ibid.*

7. *Ibid.*

8. *Ibid.*

9. *Ibid.*

10. C. Colburn Hardy, *The Investor's Guide to Technical Analysis* (McGraw-Hill, NY, 1978).

11. Sperandeo, *Trader Vic.*

12. *Ibid.*

13. Bruce Kramer, "Using Indicators in Trading Ranges and Trends," *Technical Analysis of Stocks and Commodities,* April 1994.

14. *Ibid.*

15. *Ibid.*

16. Alexander Elder, *Trading for a Living* (John Wiley & Sons, NY, 1993).

17. Appel, *Winning Market Systems.*

18. Stan Weinstein, *Secrets of Profiting in Bull and Bear Markets* (Dow Jones Irwin, Homewood, IL, 1988).

19. Arthur Sklarew, *Techniques of a Professional Commodity Chart Analyst* (Commodity Research Bureau, NY, 1980).

20. Arthur Merrill, "Stocks Above Moving Average," *Technical Analysis of Stocks and Commodities,* Vol. 8, 1990, p. 204.

21. Good discussions of support and resistance levels can be found in Hardy's *Investor's Guide to Technical Analysis,* Elder's *Trading for a Living,* and Jiler's *How Charts Can Help You in the Stock Market.* See also the standard reference books listed in reference 1.

22. Appel, *Winning Market Systems.*

23. William O'Neil, *How to Make Money in Stocks* (McGraw-Hill, NY, 1991).

24. John Dennis Brown, *Panic Profits* (McGraw-Hill, NY, 1994).

25. O'Neil, *How to Make Money in Stocks.*

26. John Murphy, *Technical Analysis of the Futures Markets* (New York Institute of Finance, NY, 1986).

27. The cup-with-handle pattern is described in detail in O'Neil, *How to Make Money in Stocks,* and Gregory Kuhn, "The Cup-with-Handle Pattern," *Technical Analysis of Stocks and Commodities,* March 1995.

28. *Ibid.*

29. *Ibid.*

30. *Ibid.*

31. Kuhn, "The Cup-with-Handle Pattern."

32. Mamis and Mamis, *When to Sell.*

33. *Ibid.*

34. Colby and Meyers, *Encyclopedia of Technical Market Indicators.*

THE INDIVIDUAL INVESTOR'S PERSONAL LIBRARY

THE CORE COLLECTION

THE INVESTMENT PROCESS

Bernstein, Peter. *Capital Ideas* (Maxwell Macmillan International, NY, 1992)

Johnson, Mark. *The Random Walk and Beyond* (John Wiley & Sons, NY, 1988)

ECONOMIC ANALYSIS

Frumkin, Norman. *Tracking America's Economy* (M. E. Sharpe, Armonk, NY, 1992)

Galbraith, John Kenneth. *The Affluent Society* (New American Library, NY, 1984)

ANALYSIS OF STOCKS AND THEIR MARKETS

Loeb, Gerald. *The Battle for Investment Survival* (Simon & Schuster, NY, 1956)

Mamis, Justin, and Robert Mamis. *When to Sell* (Simon & Schuster, NY, 1977)

Mamis, Justin. *How to Buy* (Farrar, Straus, Giroux, NY, 1982)

Mamis, Justin. *The Nature of Risk* (Addison-Wesley, NY, 1991)

O'Neil, William. *How to Make Money in Stocks* (McGraw-Hill, NY, 1991)

Stein, Lawrence. *Value Investing* (John Wiley & Sons, NY, 1987)

MUTUAL FUNDS

Bogle, John. *Bogle on Mutual Funds* (Irwin Professional Publishing, NY, 1993)

THE SUPPLEMENTAL COLLECTION

ECONOMIC ANALYSIS

Brockway, George. *The End of Economic Man* (W. W. Norton, NY, 1993)

Heilbroner, Robert, and Lester Thurow. *Economics Explained* (Simon & Schuster, NY, 1987)

Hunt, Lacy. *A Time to Be Rich* (Rawson Associates, NY, 1987)

ANALYSIS OF STOCKS AND THEIR MARKETS

Appel, Gerald. *Winning Stock Market Systems* (Signalert Corp., Great Neck, NY, 1974)

Elder, Alexander. *Trading for a Living* (John Wiley & Sons, NY, 1993)

Fosback, Norman. *Stock Market Logic* (Dearborn Financial Publishing, 1976)

Graham, Benjamin. *The Intelligent Investor* (Harper & Row, NY, 1973)

Lefevre, Edwin. *Reminiscences of a Stock Operator* (Pocket Books, NY; reprinted 1968)

Sperendeo, Victor. *Trader Vic: Methods of a Wall Street Master* (John Wiley & Sons, NY, 1991)

Weinstein, Stan. *Secrets for Profiting in Bull and Bear Markets* (Dow Jones Irwin, Homewood, IL, 1988)

Weiss, Geraldine, and Janet Lowe. *Dividends Don't Lie* (Dearborn Financial Publishing, 1989)

Zweig, Martin. *Winning on Wall Street* (Warner Books, NY, 1990)

THE REFERENCE COLLECTION

Cottle, Sidney, Roger Murray, and Frank Block. *Graham & Dodd's Security Analysis* (McGraw-Hill, NY, 1988)

Murphy, John. *Technical Analysis of the Futures Markets* (NYIF, NY, 1986)

Pring, Martin. *Technical Analysis Explained* (McGraw-Hill, NY, 1991)

Pring, Martin. *Martin Pring on Market Momentum* (PO Box 624, Gloucester, VA 23061-0624)

INDEX

ABOUT THE AUTHOR

Dhun H. Sethna, a physician in Southern California, credits *Investor's Business Daily* as the main resource for helping him grow his portfolio. Dr. Sethna wrote *Investing Smart* with contributions from the staff of *Investor's Business Daily*.

NO POSTAGE
NECESSARY
IF MAILED
IN THE
UNITED STATES

BUSINESS REPLY MAIL
FIRST-CLASS MAIL   PERMIT NO. 71898   LOS ANGELES CA 90066

POSTAGE WILL BE PAID BY ADDRESSEE

DEPARTMENT A
INVESTOR'S BUSINESS DAILY
P O BOX 66370
LOS ANGELES CA 90099-3937

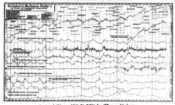

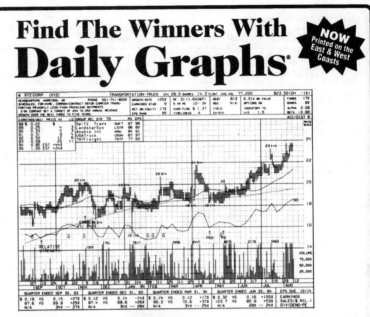